History of Computing

The History of Computing series publishes high-quality books which address the history of computing, with an emphasis on the 'externalist' view of this history, more accessible to a wider audience. The series examines content and history from four main quadrants: the history of relevant technologies, the history of the core science, the history of relevant business and economic developments, and the history of computing as it pertains to social history and societal developments.

Titles can span a variety of product types, including but not exclusively, themed volumes, biographies, 'profile' books (with brief biographies of a number of key people), expansions of workshop proceedings, general readers, scholarly expositions, titles used as ancillary textbooks, revivals and new editions of previous worthy titles.

These books will appeal, varyingly, to academics and students in computer science, history, mathematics, business and technology studies. Some titles will also directly appeal to professionals and practitioners of different backgrounds.

More information about this series at http://www.springer.com/series/8442

Douglas R. Dechow • Daniele C. Struppa
Editors

Intertwingled

The Work and Influence of Ted Nelson

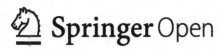

Editors
Douglas R. Dechow
Chapman University
Orange, CA, USA

Daniele C. Struppa
Chapman University
Orange, CA, USA

ISSN 2190-6831   ISSN 2190-684X   (electronic)
History of Computing
ISBN 978-3-319-36380-6   ISBN 978-3-319-16925-5   (eBook)
DOI 10.1007/978-3-319-16925-5

Springer Cham Heidelberg New York Dordrecht London

Springer International Publishing AG Switzerland is part of Springer Science+Business Media (www.
springer.com)

We humbly dedicate this book to Marlene J. Mallicoat, Ted's wife and our friend.

From *left* to *right*, Dr. Douglas R. Dechow, Dr. Ted Nelson, and Dr. Daniele C. Struppa at Nelson's honorary degree conferral

Preface

Over 40 years ago, Ted Nelson published *Computer Lib/Dream Machines*. It was a most unusual piece of writing. Its layout of two books in a single binding—published back-to-back, but reversed so that each had a front cover—was meant to confront the user's notions of text and reading. In the *Computer Lib* portion, Ted wrote, "EVERYTHING IS DEEPLY INTERTWINGLED. In an important sense there are no 'subjects' at all; there is only all knowledge, since the cross-connections among the myriad topics of this world simply cannot be divided up neatly." Ted Nelson wrote these words as a challenge to us all, a call to engage with the interconnected complexity of knowledge. We might say that Ted Nelsons' exhortation is nothing but a clear reflection of what the liberal arts are supposed to teach. Nelson's claim is maybe the strongest call for a renewed attention to what academia likes to call "interdisciplinarity," but as we read in his words, it becomes clear that the point is not to build bridges between disciplines, but rather to realize that the divide between disciplines (or 'subjects' as Nelson calls them) is artificial and intellectually cannot be sustained. Ted Nelson has spent more than 50 years making us aware of the need for and exhorting us to develop the tools that would change the world's way of seeing, accessing, and connecting information. And once we agree that disciplinary barriers need to be taken down, the whole idea behind the worldwide web becomes simply the technological realization of an intellectual decision.

On April 24, 2014, Chapman University hosted "Intertwingled: The Work and Influence of Ted Nelson," a conference to celebrate the anniversary of the publication of *Computer Lib/Dream Machines* and his many contributions to computing and to the generation of knowledge in our world. As a part of that event, Chapman University awarded Ted Nelson an honorary doctorate. We felt that such an award was most appropriate, as Ted's approach to the big questions is a reflection of our university's most esteemed hopes for our students and the embodiment of our mission: to teach our students how to lead inquiring, ethical, and productive lives as global citizens for the rest of their lives. The award citation read in part:

By focusing on the important questions of how people will work with and use information, we honor your curiosity and ingenuity as a media innovator and systems designer. From your early work that led to the creation of *hypertext* and to the *docuverse*—a world-wide network of hypertext documents—that you envisioned first, you laid the groundwork for the information ecosystem that has shaped the 21st century. We honor your perseverance and tenacity in working for nearly fifty years on the Xanadu system, your vision of the docuverse.

In this volume, which takes its name from the conference, *Intertwingled*: *The Work and Influence of Ted Nelson*, Nelson, his colleagues and contemporaries from the computing world and the scholars who continue to examine his work take up those topics that have been the subject of Nelson's frenetic and fluid mind for the past 50 years: hypertext, the docuverse, and Xanadu.

We have organized the seventeen contributed chapters into four parts: I. Artistic Contributions, II. Peer Histories, III. Hypertext & Ted Nelson-influenced Research, and IV. The Last Word. As befits Nelson's wide-ranging and interdisciplinary intellect, the first section includes a cartoon and a sequence of poems; both were created in Nelson's honor. In the section of Peer Histories, readers get a sense of the milieu that resulted from Nelson's ideas. In addition, several of the authors discuss what it is like to collaborate directly with Nelson. The penultimate section, Hypertext & Ted Nelson-influenced Research, wrestles with Nelson's influence and legacy.

The fourth and final section of *Intertwingled,* appropriately enough entitled The Last Word, is comprised of a single contribution from Ted Nelson himself. In it, he tells the reader—just as he did at the Intertwingled conference—that he's spent the day listening to his obituaries. He says, "I feel very lucky to have eavesdropped on these thoughtful pre-mortems." Nothing could be further from the truth. We believe that the world—particularly the technology world—is better off for having Ted alive and kicking at the boundaries of the possible. We can confirm that Nelson's mind is as active as ever—he constantly emails us with his observations of the world—and that his body has barely slowed.

Shortly after the Intertwingled conference, Open Xanadu had its first release, a moment 50 years in the making. Who can tell what will be next from Ted Nelson? We look forward to more years of Nelson's ground-breaking ideas and tireless work. We wish him much success as he pursues his vision of the docuverse.

Acknowledgments

The editors are grateful to the people at Springer, especially Simon Rees, Associate Editor for Computer Science, who helped bring this project to fruition and to Chapman University for sponsoring the conference and this Festschrift. We are deeply indebted to the Program Committee who organized the Intertwingled conference. In particular, we would like to thank Andy Anderson, Susanna Branch, Erika

Curiel, Laurie Cussalli, Mando Diaz, Rebecca Green, Sheri Ledbetter, David Lowe, Carl Minor, and Frank Warren. In addition, members of the Chapman University Department of English assisted in producing the Festschrift; graduate students Danny De Maio and Tatiana Servin transcribed several of the talks, and Dr. Anna Leahy provided editing for those talks.

Orange, CA   Douglas R. Dechow
February 7, 2015   Daniele C. Struppa

Contents

Part IV   The Last Word

Contributors

Robert M. Akscyn Knowledge Systems, Las Vegas, NV, USA

Belinda Barnet Media and Communications, Faculty of Health, Arts and Design, School of Arts, Social Sciences and Humanities, Department of Media and Communication, Swinburne University of Technology, Hawthorn, Australia

Christine L. Borgman Department of Information Studies, University of California, Los Angeles, CA, USA

Douglas R. Dechow Chapman University, Orange, CA, USA

Wendy Hall Web Science Institute, University of Southampton, Southampton, UK

Frode Hegland London, UK

Dick Heiser Los Angeles, CA, USA

Brewster Kahle Internet Archive, San Francisco, CA, USA

Alan Kay Viewpoints Research Institute, Los Angeles, CA, USA

Ken Knowlton Retired. Formerly, Bell Laboratories' Inc., Sarasota, FL, USA

Henry Lowood Stanford University Libraries, Stanford, CA, USA

Theodor Holm Nelson Project Xanadu, Sausalito, CA, USA

Andrew Pam Project Xanadu, Croydon, VIC, Australia

Daniel Rosenberg Clark Honors College, University of Oregon, Eugene, OR, USA

Peter Schmideg (deceased)

Ben Shneiderman Department of Computer Science, A. V. Williams Building, University of Maryland, Bethesda, MD, USA

Laurie Spiegel New York, NY, USA

Daniele C. Struppa Chapman University, Orange, CA, USA

Ed Subitzky (deceased)

Noah Wardrip-Fruin Department of Computational Media, University of California, Santa Cruz, CA, USA

Part I
Artistic Contributions

Chapter 1
The Computer Age

Ed Subitzky

E. Subitzky (✉)

© The Author(s) 2015
D.R. Dechow, D.C. Struppa (eds.), *Intertwingled*, History of Computing,
DOI 10.1007/978-3-319-16925-5_1

3

Cartoonist and humor writer

Chapter 2
Odes to Ted Nelson

Ben Shneiderman

2.1 Intertwingling

Ted Nelson's intertwingled brains,
Spawn repeating rhythmic trains
Telling stories in poetic scenes
From ComputerLib and Dream Machines.
His restless mind reveals a lyric vision
Shining brightly with intense precision.

His playful, play-filled frantic imagery
Expands my mind with his skullduggery
Masquerading as intended trickery
But always making planful mockery
Of those who believe in standard crockery.
Oh this must sound like jabberwockery.

But honestly I speak without temerity.
I merely wish to add to his celebrity
And honor him for his celerity
A joyful sprite of youthful clarity.

B. Shneiderman (✉)
Department of Computer Science, A. V. Williams Building,
University of Maryland, College Park, MD 20742, USA
e-mail: ben@cs.umd.edu

D.R. Dechow, D.C. Struppa (eds.), *Intertwingled*, History of Computing,
DOI 10.1007/978-3-319-16925-5_2

2.2   Playful Mayhem

Playful mayhem
Slippery fun to invent words that capture bold ideas
Sworfing flinks transclude reality
Twinkling, awesome Nelson
Transpire, conspire, inspire
Transclude, conclude, include
Persistent commitment to
A life with one clear purpose
Ever-connecting hypermind

Ted's never met a limit he didn't want to break
He's never found a rule he didn't want to fake.

Self-confident clarity, true to his beliefs
Original visions, zigging-zagging
Fresh humping, bumping
To what Markoff called "his grander ideals"

2.3   Early Admiration

My earliest description of Ted Nelson was on the 1988 ACM disk *Hypertext on Hypertext*, which was the first electronic journal, incorporating the articles from the July 1988 issue of *Communications of the ACM*. These articles were derived from the 1987 Hypertext conference. We created the articles as hypertext documents using our HyperTies system (www.cs.umd.edu/hcil/hyperties). The tilde marks (~) surround phrases that were highlighted selectable links that could be clicked on to jump to the related article.

Our research and development were inspired by Vannevar Bush's 1945 description of Memex, in which links were numeric codes that had to be typed in and by Ted Nelson's work with Andries Van Dam. Only later did we see Doug Engelbart's 1968 demo video, which had selectable list items. So while there were several precedents, I take credit for the highlighted textual link embedded in sentences. I invented the highlighted textual link in 1984, while working with grad student Dan Ostroff, as part of our development of an electronic encyclopedia for the emerging U.S. Holocaust Memorial Museum. We ran empirical studies of different highlighting schemes and tested user capacity to navigate as well as ability to comprehend the paragraphs of text. We called the highlighted textual links, "embedded menus," but Tim Berners-Lee referred to them with the more compelling term "hot spots" in citing our work in his spring 1989 manifesto for the web.

Fig. 2.1 Example image of Ted Nelson in hyperties system [1]

A pioneering visionary of universal hypertext systems including the social and legal structures; keynote speaker at Hypertext '87 Workshop.

Ted Nelson (See Fig. 2.1)
Keynote Speaker at Hypertext '87 Workshop.

Ted Nelson's creative visions are amply displayed in his lively books, *Computer Lib/Dream Machines* and *Literary Machines*, which detail his hypertext vision. Nelson understood that major social and legal changes would be necessary to realize his concept of universal hypertext environment. His XANADU system supported enormous docuverses including complex links among literary sources, quotations, critiques, etc. and a vast global network accessible from community-oriented computer centers.

Nelson worked with the hypertext group at Brown University and collaborated with Andries Van Dam in the 1970s. Ted Nelson was one of the three keynote speakers at the Hypertext 87 Workshop. Recently AutoCAD, Inc. initiated a collaboration with Nelson and his Xanadu project.

2.4 Second Admiration

A year later I wrote about Ted Nelson for the world's first electronic book [2], as determined by our Library of Congress colleagues asking for guidance about how to catalog it.

Ted Nelson's Xanadu.

The first to coin the terms *hypertext* and *hypermedia* in his book *Dream Machines*.

In his book "Dream Machines," Nelson developed his ideas about augmentation with an emphasis on creating a global, unified literary environment. This environment looked beyond simple hierarchical relations to a densely interwoven network of nodes which would reflect the ideas within the human mind. His hypertext system, Xanadu, was in fact to be a network of interconnected hypertext engines used as an environment for both cooperative thinking and the electronic publication of hypertext works.

2.5 Photos at Oxford Internet Institute

My photos of Ted Nelson (Figs. 2.2 and 2.3) show him to be cheerful and ready for creativity.

Fig. 2.2 Ted Nelson, Jennifer Preece, and Marlene Mallicoat at Oxford Internet Institute in June 2006. Ted has his colored pens ready for action

Fig. 2.3 Ted Nelson and author at Oxford Internet Institute in June 2006. Author is trying to show that Ted Nelson is number one

References

1. Shneiderman B (1988) Hypertext on hypertext (Distributed on hyperties disk with 1Mbyte data and graphics incorporating). Communications of the ACM, ACM Press, New York
2. Shneiderman B, Kearsley G (1989) Hypertext hands-on!: an introduction to a new way of organizing and accessing information. Addison-Wesley, Reading world's first electronic book

Part II
Peer Histories

Chapter 3
The Two-Eyed Man

Alan Kay

I was unable to be at Chapman University for the celebration of Ted Nelson's life's work, so Bonnie MacBird and I made this video to celebrate your day.[1] We wanted to thank Ted for his role in us meeting up, falling in love, and getting married. In the video, Bonnie explains:

> This is how Ted Nelson spawned the movie Tron and a marriage that's lasted more than thirty years. The year was 1979. I'd just left Universal Studios to write a movie about a video game warrior inside of a computer. There were no personal computers at that time [beyond] these. In L.A., there were many video arcades, but only one computer store for Home Brew-types only. I went there and found this book: *Computer Lib/Dream Machines* by Ted Nelson (Fig. 3.1).
>
> I read it cover to cover. Well, cover to middle, then upside down, and other cover to middle. There was an article about Alan Kay, so I went up to Xerox PARC and met the guy. A half hour meeting stretched into hours and Alan Kay became the technical consultant on the movie *Tron*. We spent many happy hours in conversation along Venice and Santa Monica beaches. I wrote a script filled with "cool" science. There was a bit who wanted to be a program, and there was a video game warrior who wanted to be a human. The script was uploaded to PARC, and then I went up there and edited the script on the Alto computer, making *Tron* the first movie script ever to be edited using a Word Processing program. It sold to Disney and after eight new writers and considerable meddling it became the movie *Tron*. Groundbreaking, yes, but Alan and I think the marriage turned out better than the movie! We thank you, Ted Nelson.

As Thorton Wilder's old fortune-teller says, "It is easy to tell the future," but asks "who can tell the past?" It's not just a memory problem, but one of too much complicated detail without enough perspective. It would be great if we could go back and look at the world Bonnie talks about, and, to some extent, we can.

---

[1] This chapter has been transcribed and edited from a video created for the Intertwingled conference (Alan Kay Talk at Ted Nelson Tribute: https://www.youtube.com/watch?v=AnrlSqtpOkw).

A. Kay (✉)
Viewpoints Research Institute, Los Angeles, CA, USA
e-mail: alan@vpri.org

D.R. Dechow, D.C. Struppa (eds.), *Intertwingled*, History of Computing,
DOI 10.1007/978-3-319-16925-5_3

Fig. 3.1 Bonnie MacBird with a copy of Ted Nelson's *Computer Lib/Dream Machines*

Some years ago, Xerox decided to clean its warehouse and throw out most of the PARC data disks.

Roughly one hundred disks out of thousands were rescued, and a few thousand files were recovered. A single one of all those files happened to contain one of our systems from the 1970s (Fig. 3.2). Smalltalk was completely self-contained. There's no separate operating system, applications, etc., only software computers communicating with each other and each simulating some aspect of the personal computer system. Some objects simulate characters on the screen; some simulate pictures; some, windows; some, places where the users can do things.

The software computers are, in terms of virtual hardware, independent of the physical computers they run on. To bring this back to life, we emulated the virtual hardware in Javascript. It is faster than the actual PARC computers of 40 years ago! With this approach, we have a time machine that allows us to go back, back, back into the past and run the same software that both Bonnie and Steve Jobs saw.

In Fig. 3.3, we see familiar forms: overlapping windows, iconic representations, and so forth. Windows are objects that are *views* of objects: tools and the kinds of resources that media authors use to create the writings of the future. They're not stovepiped "apps." You can bring any and all objects in the Smalltalk system to any of these projects. For example, here we see a view of the system itself and animation. A half-tone painting I did 40 years ago. I can scribble it up a little bit for you. Here's some text. This system also had a gesture recognizer.

Now let's go to the project where I organized this talk. In Fig. 3.4, we see many small windows that look unto projects of their own. We can think of this system as having unlimited "desktops" on which "projects" can be done, and all the resources needed for each project can be brought there and they'll persist over time.

The Xerox E-Dump!

Fig. 3.2 A hard drive (location shown in *circle*) containing a Smalltalk image from the 1970s was retrieved from the digital trash heap

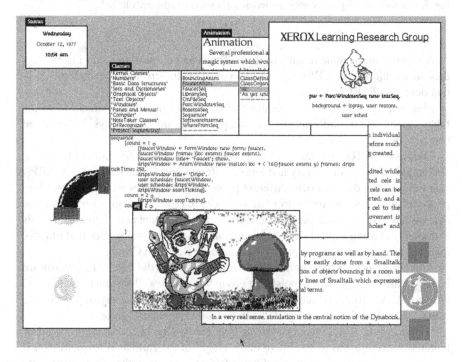

Fig. 3.3 Image of a Smalltalk screen at Xerox PARC in the 1970s

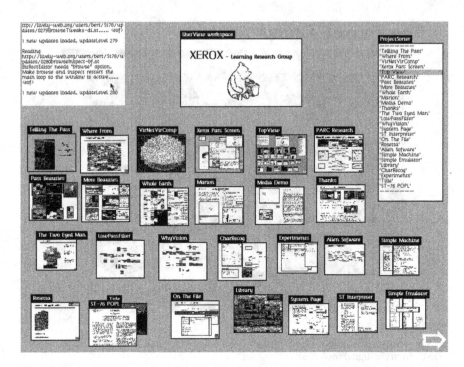

Fig. 3.4 Screen showing many project windows. They can be arbitrarily linked

Anything can be done in each of them. They can be linked together in any way; they are not hierarchical. I'll enter one—a typical media screen (shown in Fig. 3.5)—that describes PARC.

This work was part of the "elephant of personal computing," which, as in the fable of the blind philosophers, is interpreted in different ways by different researchers.

The ARPA IPTO (Advanced Projects Research Agency Information Processing Techniques Office) community had lots of different views. The basic idea of ARPA was to avoid the disputes over different points of view that were part of the blind philosopher's fable and try to do what scientists have done to figure out a universe that we can only approach piecemeal. PARC was an offshoot and microcosm of this community starting in the 1970s, and individual researchers were often part of more than one research area. I was part of the Learning Research Group.

Another group was the Computer Systems Lab, which did much of the hardware heavy-lifting and day-to-day tools. One group that is less well-known is the POLOS Group (PARC OnLine Office Systems), which was made from some of people who came over to PARC in the early 1970s from Doug Engelbart's group.

A myth about PARC was its extreme originality. One of the triumphs of a few hundred years ago was to be able to make globes of the earth as if it would look if we were out in space. Two hundred years later, the views in the 1980s were quite

Four of Parc's Computer Research "Emphases"

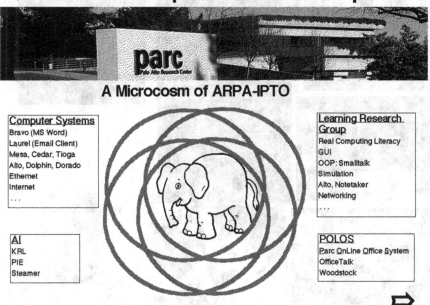

A Microcosm of ARPA-IPTO

Computer Systems
Bravo (MS Word)
Laurel (Email Client)
Mesa, Cedar, Tioga
Alto, Dolphin, Dorado
Ethernet
Internet
. . .

Learning Research Group
Real Computing Literacy
GUI
OOP: Smalltalk
Simulation
Alto, Notetaker
Networking
. . .

AI
KRL
PIE
Steamer

POLOS
Parc OnLine Office System
OfficeTalk
Woodstock

Fig. 3.5 Some of the many facets of the invention of personal computing at Xerox PARC

identical to the globes of 1780. There were hardly any surprises. Likewise, it is, perhaps, more accurate to claim that we in PARC were less original in the 1970s than we had been in the 1960s when many of the ideas were invented and explored for the first time (Fig. 3.6).

In the early 1960s, there was an enormous wealth of ways to think about personal computing and networks, including Sketchpad, the very image of personal computing. Some of the personal computing explorers included Douglas Engelbart, of course, and Ted Nelson and Andy van Dam. The Grail Gesture Recognition System on a tablet that was invented the same year as the mouse—1964—and the conventions of making arrows, windows, and so on, including moving and resizing them. All of this was happening at that time: Seymour Papert with his Logo programming language and Turtle graphics; Simula; and some of our own stuff as well, such as the Arpanet, the Flex Machine and its first object-oriented operating system, the idea of Dynabook, and much, much more. It was an exciting time.

The *Whole Earth Catalog* and its folks were nearby in Menlo Park thinking big thoughts about universal access to tools. Not just physical, but especially mental. This was the first book in the PARC library, and it had a big influence on how we thought things should be. We loved the idea of lots of different tools being available with explanations and comments, and we could see that it would be just wonderful if such media could be brought to life as one found and made it. This thinking led to

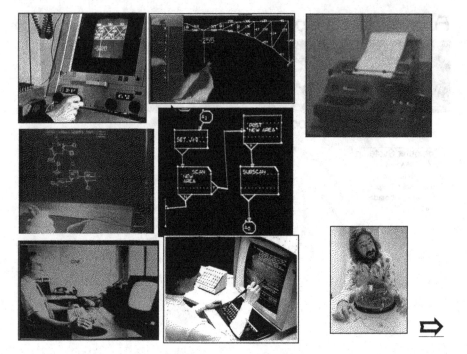

Fig. 3.6 Some of the precursors of the work at Xerox PARC

ideas of how to explain and explore by actually making things from computer stuff in the kind of general literacy we have for reading and writing. Now, we could include the reading and writing of dynamic models. This kind of literacy is best learned by children, so we started to work with them.

In my conference presentation, I showed the computer version of an article that 13-year-old Marian Goldeen wrote in *Creative Computing Magazine* in 1975 about what she'd done the previous year in our group. The computer version goes beyond reading to allow the reader to try out the very things that Marian is talking about. We called this form an active essay (Fig. 3.7).

In the middle of the essay is a simulation of the Alto screen so one can see what things looked like in her projects and do the same things that she did. She started off by making a box object called Joe that can be sent messages to get it to behave. Programming in Smalltalk is more like training intelligent agents than it is like the more standard metaphor of a cook making something from inert ingredients.

I showed a demo we used to do that combined animation and painting tools. The animation effect depends on what the brain does when it sees two different images, one right after the other. Animators like to say that animation takes place in between the frames. This means that we'd really like to do the redrawing of the bottom frame while the animation is running. But these are different tools. In the demo, the animation tool is animating the bouncing ball, and you can see that it's a bit weak. We'd expect that the ball would deform when it hits the ground.

Adapted from
Creative Computing Magazine
April 1975

Learning About Smalltalk
by Marian Goldeen

My name is Marian Goldeen. I'm an eighth grade student at Jordan Junior High School in Palo Alto, California, and I would like to tell you about how I got started working with computers at Xerox and the class I taught.

It all started in December, 1973 when I was in the 7th grade. There were four people in my class who were interested in taking a course about the computer language Smalltalk at Xerox.

When we first started we were shown how to start the machines up and use a program that drew boxes like this. To see, type a return after ⬚ joe ← Box init below:

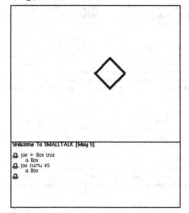

We can make joe turn, grow, shrink, and move. Try typing:
    joe turn: 45   and hit <return> to "doit"! Try:
    joe grow: 20   and:
    joe grow: ⁻15   and:
    joe moveTo: 30@50   (a position on the screen is horizontal@vertical)
We can get joe to follow the mouse pointer by typing
    joe follow
We can make different shapes by telling joe how many sides to have:
    joe sides ← 6
We can look at the way joe does its moveBu: action.

What if we don't do the "undraw"? This should leave the marks from the previous position behind. This could make a paint brush if you could hook it to the mouse!

```
moveTo: loc
    [self undraw.
     self placeAt: loc.
     self draw]
```

Here is the painting program I made from many different kinds of box shapes, with menus for the shapes and the "paint".

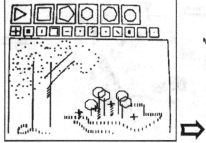

Fig. 3.7 Image of Marion Goldeen's "active essay" article for *Creative Computing* magazine

If there were apps in a commercial version of personal computing, we'd most likely expect that they don't talk to each other and it would be difficult to get them to talk to each other. This is a pet peeve of Ted's. But in this animation, they are just objects, and any object can talk to any object.

I'll take a look at the menu of the animation window. We can stop it ticking, and we can single-step the frame we care about. Maybe we want to share this frame with a painting tool. If this was prepared ahead of time, it would already be done. Instead, to paraphrase Thoreau, we need to find out what Texas might have to say to Massachusetts; that is, how did each of the tools characterize their parts and behaviors. Then we can do what Ted loves, shown in Fig. 3.8, which is to draw a line between the two windows. Some of the actions can be pre-defined, but we can also define one later by doing this gesture to create a dynamic link between the two windows. The painter's picture wants to be linked to the bouncing window's current frame, so we just write that in there and do it. The animation can be started again, and I can start painting the deformed ball. In the end, it starts to look pretty good. To prepare for the conference presentation, we had a terrific time bringing this old system back to life over the previous few months.

All the demos and forms I used in my talk were derived from old examples shown and published in the 1970s and made without changing Smalltalk's graphic system. The beautiful one-bit pictures use the Floyd-Steinberg technique, which

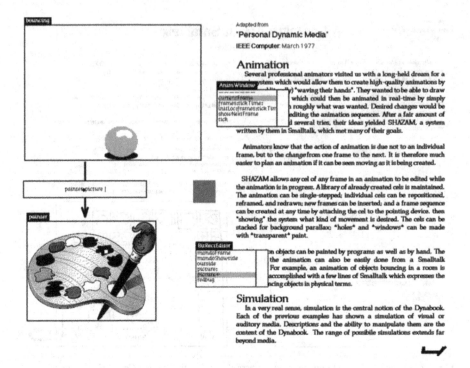

Fig. 3.8 Smalltalk demonstration of a dynamic connection between two windows

was worked out at Stanford and PARC at the same time our system was built. But back then, we hardly used pictures like these, or many bit-map paintings because there simply wasn't enough storage to hold them. It's nice to take advantage of the larger storage capacities today. An iPhone's storage, for example, is many tens of thousands times larger and faster than the PARC machines.

An ancient proverb says that, in the country of the blind, the one-eyed man is king. Robert Heinlein's version of this proverb is that, in the country of the blind, the one-eyed man is in for one hell of a rough time! My version is that, in the country of blind, the one-eyed people run things and the two-eyed people are in for one hell of a rough time. That said, we owe much of civilization to the insights and suffering of the tiny number of two-eyed people. Ted Nelson was one of those few two-eyed people. We owe much to him, and this is being celebrated in this collection of essays.

A two-eyed person—Ted Nelson—comes up with a glorious symphony of how life will be so much deeper and richer if we just did *X*, but the regular world acts as a low-pass filter on the ideas. In the end, he is lucky to get a dial tone. The blind won't see it, and the one-eyed people will only catch a glimpse, but all of them think their sense or glimpse of the elephant is the whole thing. In our day and age, if they think money can be made from their glimpse, something will happen. They want to sell to the mass market of the blind so they will narrow the glimpse down even more. They could be educators and help the blind learn how to see; this is what science has done for the entire human race. But learning to see is a chore, so most, especially marketing people, are not interested. This is too bad, especially when we consider the efforts the two-eyed people like Ted have to go through to even have a glimpse happen. One of the keys is for the two-eyed people to turn into evangelists. Both Ted and our mutual hero, Douglas Engelbart, worked tirelessly over their lifetimes to point out that, in this dial-tone world, the emperor not only has no clothes but his cell phone can't transmit real music. Yes, I've mixed a metaphor or two.

Another key is to make a working system of the future. This was ARPA's and especially PARC's main mission. Make something that works, not just for a demo, but for a group of people. Some of what I showed during my talk is what Steve Jobs saw, and the Macintosh was a result of his glimpse and also interpretations of that glimpse by him and others at Apple. But it missed a number of really important ideas. Many of Ted's and Doug's ideas have been missed.

So, with all this working against someone like Ted, why bother having visions? Standard schooling is already trying to convert two-eyed children into standard children, that is, into blind children. Why not just put more effort into this and save all the bother?

To me, the visionaries are the most important people we have because it is only by comparing their ideas with our normal ideas that we can gauge how we are doing. Otherwise, as it is for most people, normal becomes reality, and they only measure from that less broad view of reality. Toss Ted back into this mix, and you've upset the Apple cart—and that's what we need! This allows us to see that normal is only one of many possible constructions of reality, and some of them could have been much better. In addition, the normal ideas in the future could be very different and much better from what is considered reality today.

Let's be very thankful that we live in a place where two-eyed people were really supported in the 1960s and at least tolerated today. And let us also be thankful that we have a two-eyed person like Ted Nelson who has been tirelessly energetic about not just having ideas but also about going out and telling people about those ideas, not letting them die, not letting them get absorbed into the low-pass filter.

Chapter 4
Ted Nelson's Xanadu

Caution – Four Letter Words Ahead

Ken Knowlton

Ted Nelson has a wide personal history of meeting writers, folks in the performing arts, and computer geeks who have brought us the modern flood of so-called "information." By 1974 he had met, as shown by *Computer Lib/Dream Machines*, a dozen times as many people in computerdom as I had. Since then, his interest and energy for collecting ideas and methods has continued undaunted. In normal conversation, it isn't unusual for him to pull a pad from his shirt pocket and begin scribbling. I presume he's capturing something brilliant or stupid that I just said.

He has a box-car-size trove of books, notes, correspondence, files, manuals, and related debris gleaned from our culture's thoughts and toys. Somehow he got his arms and mind sufficiently around the tangled middens to write his breezy *Geeks Bearing Gifts*. The book is a compendium of everything you did (or didn't) want to know about the exciting (or dismal) uses (or misuses) of computers. It is also judiciously spiced with attitude.

We've been friends for many years, in spite of—perhaps, because of—the fact that we haven't really worked together. We do have similar reactions, I believe, to the how-to-live attitude of Spinoza who said:

> I have striven
> not to laugh at human actions,
> not to weep at them,
> nor to hate them,
> but to understand them.

On this four point check-up, my scoring for both of us is the same: 25 %. We fail badly on the first three, and we do well with the fourth. We do laugh at the world, but, it's with a tart sense of humor. What else can one do when so many people seem intentionally insane? We don't exactly cry, but we despair at human over-reach. In *Computer Lib/Dream Machines*, Ted bemoaned the combination of overpopulation

K. Knowlton (✉)
Retired. Formerly, Bell Laboratories, Inc., Sarasota, FL 34232, USA
e-mail: kckmosaics@aol.com

© The Author(s) 2015
D.R. Dechow, D.C. Struppa (eds.), *Intertwingled*, History of Computing,
DOI 10.1007/978-3-319-16925-5_4

and resource depletion. Hate is not too strong for those who—in striving for fame, wealth, and/or power—are so insouciantly and widely destructive.

We do agree with striving to understand the world, and Ted pursues this with great energy and devotion. He also tries to arrange for folks in general to better understand people's stories and their intertwined connections.

In short, better arrangements for understanding have been his life-long concern and quest. He has sought answers to the following: (1) what tangible stuff ought to be attended to; (2) how should it to be organized; (3) with what grappling tools; and (4) should we want to do what?

A Hint: Some Four-Letter Words For thousands of years, people have left records of things important to them: myths, legends, morals, customs, laws, fairy tales, plays, paintings, sculpture, songs, movies, pageants, and operas. Each record was a statement about themselves and their outward and inward experiences. Run through the alphabet slowly, with a small sample of short words, and ask about each: "What is evoked that should be recorded?"

> Acta, Book, Copy, Data, Echo, Fact, Game, Hope, Idea,
> Joke, Know, Laws, Myth, Note, Oral, Page, Quip, Role,
> Song, Text, Uses, View, Want, Xray, Yore, Zone

We can hardly speak three sentences without alluding to something about us that's been/being preserved. The creation of a modern Library of Alexandria— and ways to benefit from it—is a mind-boggler.

Once you go beyond the process of collecting, it becomes necessary to begin the process of "understanding." We hope that those who follow will study, search, read, and try to make sense of who and what we were. And if "we" is more than tekkies, or Americans, or modern humans, then how did "we" relate to the others? Nothing arrives *de novo*. Almost everything one says or writes has lines of descent to it. Polite and diligent authors make such references explicit with quote marks and footnotes.

Here are a couple of examples for consideration. How to we trace the relationships in a letter-to-the-editor that corrects a statement in a review of two different authors' translations into English of some odd ancient work. In my current life, I performed the following query in Google: "Knowlton's Fast Storage Allocator." This is a two-page paper that I wrote while at formerly Bell Telephone Laboratories, Inc [1]. Google responded with a list of 27,000 hits. If I search for "Ted Nelson," Google's response starts with "45,000,000"! What do those numbers mean? This is a set of connections of some sort, but they are quite unmanageable.

Here we have design issues galore! How many categories of items are present? What are the relationships: pointers to entireties, parts, paraphrases, allusions, hearsay, forerunners, anticipated future works, or other parts of the same text? Can pointers be permanent, tentative, private, one-way, or to other pointers? Can they be grouped in sets? The list goes on and on.

What then can we say about implementation? How should this look to the user? What are the necessary tools, and what level of sophistication is required?[1] The

---

[1] System builders will be still on the scene because their job will never be finished.

system must feasible, maintainable, understandable, and the data—of course—must be correctable, updatable, and protectable.

It must also be scaleable. Imagine a small information "package" for your home office, expandable to, or part of, a larger one for the franchise office. The latter package is associated with corporate headquarters and is, or will be, mingled into the whole world. At every level, the appropriate permissions and payments must be present.

From the bottom up, what are the appropriate tools to manage this commingled complexity? Another list of short words that hint at intellectual and electronic tools:

Alfa, Baud, Code, Disk, Else, File, Grid, Hunt, Item,
Join, Keep, List, Move, Name, Omit, Path, Quit, Root,
Sort, Tree, Undo, Vary, Webs, Xout, Yoke, Zoom

Of course, there are thousands more words that apply. Should we worry? There are lots of people who already have done groundwork in information input, processing, storage, transmission, retrieval and display. That's a beginning. But it's hardly the solution.

From my own experience in putting together programming languages, one hopes for some rest and gratification at the end. But it doesn't come easily, and it's not guaranteed. Sometimes the jungle is too large, tangled, and forbidding. It's the kind of place that only the brave even dare enter.

And there's a kind of private pain that most outsiders never realize. It's the pain of trimming back, leaving out, and simplifying. It's the pressure of the bank account running low and that hooded fellow with the scythe. He's behind a bush somewhere, and he's sneaking ever closer. The really nasty part is the many things that should have been there, but along the way, really good ideas—often half-way-worked out plans and methods—got dumped. There will be no jazz funeral for them. At most, they will receive a small private tear or two. The philosopher Peit Hein was famous for his short poems he called *grooks*. Ted's situation calls to mind this particular grook:

Problems worthy
    of attack
prove their worth by
    hitting back.

There's one real difference between Ted Nelson and myself. I've been rambling for the past 50 years, picking low-hanging fruit in computer software, hardware, and art. In this same time, Ted has stuck with one gargantuan, significant, and tough problem. I marvel at this, and I commend him for it.

Summing Up, and a Puzzle Here's a puzzle, and I introduce it by noting that Ted and I have an experience in common. We each spent long stretches of our early years on a small farm. We experienced the smell of cut hay, trees to climb, animals in the woods, birds that visited for the warm months, and snow to shovel in the winter. These boyhood experiences were our springboards into an ever rich and vibrant world. Or at least, one would have thought that this would be the case. But this world is now being fried, drowned, poisoned, and overrun. It's hard to imagine, but in my own lifetime, the number of people on this planet has tripled!

Here is the puzzle. Why have we expended all of this personal effort, when we're already convinced that this whole ship of civilization is headed for the rocks? Ted said in 1974 that our ecology was in bad shape and very likely to get much worse. I urge you to read again the ending of *Computer Lib/Dream Machines*. Later, I wrote my own independent, but similar scribbles, "Great Day in the Evening" [2] and "Brief Manifesto" [3].

What record of our doings will, in any sense, last? Unlike our friend Laurie Spiegel,[2] we have no computer music, nor anything else, on the Golden Record of Voyager 1, which is traveling outside the solar system and on course to outlast the sun.

My own answer to why-all-the-effort, not for everyone, recalls what I've heard about the two types of mathematicians. Those who believe in God, say that God has a *Book* that holds all mathematical truths; those who do not think and feel in terms of God nevertheless say that such a *Book* exists!

I believe in a similar *Book*, a book of All Things that have happened, probably the one in which Omar Khayyam's imagined finger "writes, and having writ moves on." This is a book with an ever growing total history, and it includes people's hopes, values, and things they cared about. It records those things that always will have been hoped, that always will have been valued, and that always will have been cared about. Each of us has a good bit written there. Here's my toast to Ted Nelson: You have already contributed a solid and admirable chunk to that story. You are on a good track, Ted. Carry on!

References

1. Knowlton KC (1965) A fast storage allocator. Commun ACM 8(10):623–624
2. Knowlton KC (1996) Great day in the evening. The website for Ken Knowlton. http://kenknowlton.com/pages/08evening.htm. Accessed 4 Jan 2015
3. Knowlton KC (2012) Brief Manifesto. The website for Ken Knowlton. http://kenknowlton.com/pages/35manifesto.htm. Accessed 4 Jan 2015

---

[2] See in this volume, Laurie Spiegel, Chap. 6: *Riffing on Ted Nelson.*

Chapter 5
Hanging Out with Ted Nelson

Brewster Kahle

It's a great honor to honor a great man like Ted Nelson. I have very much enjoyed my whole relationship with him. That's why I've titled my short piece "Hanging Out with Ted Nelson" so that I can discuss what it is it like to sort of bum around and hitch rides and just play around with Ted. Two stories illustrate day-to-day life with a man who has, basically, put in place a lot of the infrastructure upon which my whole career has been built.

The first was meeting him. In the mid-1990s, I was working on a system to publish over the Internet so that anybody could publish or be a publisher and be seen over this wide area network. To build this system, I, of course, studied up on Vannevar Bush and the works and ideas of Bill Dunn, the lesser-sung hero of the information age who ran the Dow Jones Information Services Group. He came up with the term "metadata" and not only understood that it was the important thing, but also said it was more important than the information itself.

Then, of course, there's Ted Nelson whose works I, of course, read. I understood a lot of the ideas behind his writing and finally got the opportunity to meet Ted in an informal setting. I think it was in a cafe in Cambridge, Massachusetts. We got to hang out for a while, and I was struck by the way I approached this conversation: I am finally going to meld minds with one of the greats, and I've got some things to say that make sense. But the problem in the whole conversation was that, with a lot of the things that I was working on—the publishing systems, the archiving systems—he said, "of course you need those, but that wasn't really the point." And it was a little, I would say, disheartening. But Ted did not say this in a negative way, as when towering men sort of dice you down to size. It was that we were talking past each other, and I came away trying to figure out why that was.

I was building a system that I think has a lot of the same characteristics of what the web became, but why was he saying something quite different from what is,

B. Kahle (✉)
Internet Archive, 300 Funston Ave, 94118 San Francisco, CA, USA
e-mail: brewster@archive.org

© The Author(s) 2015
D.R. Dechow, D.C. Struppa (eds.), *Intertwingled*, History of Computing,
DOI 10.1007/978-3-319-16925-5_5

from what we had been working on for so many years—I finally figured it out, at least I think so.

Ted was building a system for writers to express the complexity of thought and a system to express the complexity of his own mind, but I had been building a reader's system, a system for people to find information no matter where they were in the world. For me, the complexity was in the finding, but maybe not in the information itself.

Ted Nelson had versions built into his system. Of course, you have to have an archive to be able to make the hypertext system work, what with all its versioning as well as the cut-and-paste across documents, so it seemed like an obvious thing to me. But Ted had another insight, one that expressed where he wanted to go, expressed things over time, one in which people could manipulate time smoothly and as easily as reading in the present. That insight was kind of a big idea. It was part and parcel to what was necessary in his world. I came to understand it as an edit-decision list, taking the continuous playing of our lives, picking it up, moving and reshaping it, and even reordering it. This idea came from the movie world rather than from the text world. But I came away from this conversation enlightened, hopeful, spurred on to do even more.

We had talked past each other, but I realized we'd built a reading machine, which I'd say is what the World Wide Web with search engines has become. We really need a writers' machine, one that would be worthy of the vision of Ted. I could have been crushed, but the conversation was an inspiration to keep moving forward. We should not say, "Hurray! We've already done it. Look at all these users." Ted doesn't say that.

Ted started hanging around at the Internet Archive because he lives in Sausalito on a cute little houseboat with wonderful Marlene. We would be hanging out and he'd be yearning to try and get more of his ideas built. He was never comfortable with saying, "Oh yes, I've achieved great things. Aren't I terrific? Now it's time for me to hang out on my houseboat." He wanted more things done.

There's this concept of these hack days or hacker-fests where people would work for a couple days, and the lore is that great things would come out of these 2-day sessions. I would always have my little doubts of how much you could actually get done in such a short amount of time. So I posed to Ted, "How about having Ted Nelson month?" I suggested we gather together a set of programmers and a set of facilities with the Internet Archive, or at least as much as we could spare. It would be his oyster for a month.

He's always audio-recording, ever since the 1960s. What would he do with a group that could scan his tapes or go build that together into something else? Or scan the books that he's written or books that he's enjoyed? I wanted to know, if he could choose a project for such a group, what would it be? He didn't want to go backwards. He didn't want to go back through his tapes. He wanted to go forward. He wanted to build ZigZag.

I was able to recruit top people that wanted to work with Ted for a month to try to crank out his new idea. He didn't want anything old. He wanted the new. So, it was Art Medlar and Jeff Ventrella, who had built 3-D worlds. There was also

Edward Betts, and there was Ted Nelson. All of them were locked in a room to build as great a system as they could in a month. It was fun to see this team go back and forth and flexibly trade off features and come up with ideas and really do a collaborative project together. This was a true collaboration that was able, by the end of this month, to come up with a demo of this different and new way of navigating data.

I have to say that this new way of navigating was too abstract for me to really understand. Of course, Ted had it all mapped out in his head. I recognized that it was very useful, but without a demonstration, I couldn't really grasp it. He probably had been living in ZigZag land for a better part of his life, but I could not understand it until this demo came out. Only then could I understand how easy it was to move and manipulate and play in space, in data with this ingenious way of moving around.

So in Ted, we have a fun and interesting guy who is funny, but who is also able to work with others. He has a willingness to refold and re-jigger, to see what it is that could be done within a short period of time.

Ted was able to make friends. Real friends. With people in every decade of their lives. This isn't easy. At least, I find that I am locked in my own decade much more than I would like. Yet Ted would form real friendships with people twenty, thirty, forty years younger than he was.

In fact, Ted and my 16-year-old son Logan became quite good friends, and he has invited Logan to spend a week with Marlene and him on the farm in New Jersey. Logan can go and hang around Ted to learn things and look at birds. They'll just generally have a good time together. The idea of having a friend across generations requires a deep respect for how other people think and what you can learn from all sorts of people.

My hat is off to Ted. I love him dearly, and I look forward to hanging around with Ted for decades to come.

Chapter 6
Riffing on Ted Nelson—Hypermind

Peter Schmideg and Laurie Spiegel

PS:

After taking a computer course at Harvard in 1960 Ted Nelson began a mystical journey. He started exploring the possibility of liberating text from paper, of developing a means whereby writers could harness text in a manner closer to human cognitive patterns: i.e., the way words flowed through our minds. In 1965 Nelson coined the term hypertext. Ultimately, in his brilliant 1974 book, *Computer Lib/ Dream Machines,* he laid down the foundation for a communications theory transcending text. Hypertext became hypermedia. Imagery and sound played roles equal to text. Nelson realized that personal computers with multimedia capabilities must burst the boundaries of artistically rendering internal reflection.

   LS:

It all started with Ted's being a thinker as well as a writer. Literature, as it existed, was constrained by its pre-written form, by the voice, by the mouth, by our one mouth into von Neuman-esque single-file, one-word at a time sequences, not the way thoughts, words, ideas swarmed in parallels, groups, flocks, words and ideas associating, intermixing and dancing in counterpoint in Ted's mind. How to write

---

Peter Schmideg was an actor, writer, director, and a radio personality. Laurie Spiegel is an electronic music pioneer and the creator of Music Mouse.

Note: I constructed this asynchronous conversation in 2014, interposing my comments into transcription excerpts of a telephone interview of Ted Nelson by Peter Schmideg recorded August. 2, 2000 as they appeared on Peter's illuminationgallery.net website's Ted Nelson web page, to simulate the kind of conversation the three of us many times experienced in person together as friends. Each bit of "dialogue" is tagged with the initials of the speaker: LS for Laurie Spiegel, PS for Peter Schmideg, and TN for Ted Nelson. Sections culled from an interview with Ted Nelson are bolded. – LS

P. Schmideg (deceased)

L. Spiegel (✉)
New York, NY 10013, USA
e-mail: laurie@xanadu.net

© The Author(s) 2015

D.R. Dechow, D.C. Struppa (eds.), *Intertwingled*, History of Computing,
DOI 10.1007/978-3-319-16925-5_6

that, and capture more of the mind in written literature? How to embody actual thought process in language? Clearly more dimensions would need to be added to conventional sequential text. There would need to be a new way of writing for a new kind of literature, but flat paper would never be able to accommodate it. So don't forget that other book of his, *Literary Machines*.

PS:

James Joyce and Marcel Proust, perhaps the two greatest writers of the twentieth century, struggled to make language transcend itself. Joyce's *Ulysses* and *Finnegans Wake* carry multimedia undertones. Joyce was fascinated by cinema. In 1909 he tried setting up the first chain of movie theaters in Ireland; alas, not being much of a businessman, his venture failed. The nighttown sequence in *Ulysses* is an attempt to fuse literature with cinema. Readers are walked through a surreal, tactilely visual mindspace. *Finnegans Wake* violently soups up printed text. In the reader's mind words explode into images and sounds. Marcel Proust's *Remembrance of Things Past* serves as a virtual reconstruction. To write it, Proust cloistered himself in a cork-lined room, allowed memories to overtake him. His sentences positively ripple, veer toward a truth at the edge of text, beyond language, as past events three-dimensionally enmesh themselves within the thread of his thoughts. Today *Remembrance of Things Past* would take the form of an ultimate home page, incorporating text, graphics, scanned photographs and paintings, audio, video, etc.

LS:

And a timeline. Intersensory writing, would be another great challenge. Proust even put in a soundtrack by mentioning specific musical works so they'd be playing in the reader's imagination as a sort of a soundtrack, and of course he used sensations such as odor and taste to enrich and extend what the reader experienced. But these were allusions, associations, not illuminations incorporated with what was being written as a part of the full sensorium of experience as we live it, and all word after word.

PS:

Metaphysically speaking Ted Nelson's Project Xanadu is Proust wired, electronically/digitally expanding stream of consciousness. Borrowing its name from Samuel Taylor Coleridge's unfinished poem, "Kubla Khan," which endeavored to capture an artist's dreamspace:

In Xanadu did Kubla Kahn A stately pleasure-dome decree...

Project Xanadu represents virtual liquid consciousness.

LS:

Consciousness, the experience of being alive, and the unstoppable drive to find a way to create a new medium of expression that would more fully capture and communicate and express all that traditional literature lacked – the ideas and the driven artistic need for them, not the technology, not an engineering vision or vantage point or concept, these were what unfurled Project Xanadu in Ted's mind. Ted was a young artist in search of a medium capable of capturing what no existing medium could. It was a vision, just as Coleridge's *Kubla Khan*'s Xanadu had been. But to make it usable would require technology, real physical earthly nuts-and-bolts practical engineering kinds of technology as well as much structural design work.

PS:
Electronically storing people's books, records, and communications was first proposed by Vannevar Bush at MIT in the early 1930s. "As We May Think," a 1945 essay Bush wrote for *Atlantic Monthly*, made the idea more generally known. Bush's concept, Memex, was a sophisticated combination of microfilm and micro-photography. It would be years before computer technology caught up with Bush, years before microfilm ceased to be the primary non-paper medium for storing text and images.

LS:
And even those then-wonderfully-futuristic visions of electronic storage lacked more than the most rudimentary cross-associative intersensual multidimensional parallelistic interconnectable multipath structures of the way the mind thinks. But it was a start, and certainly closer to the Xanadu of experiential media than plain text as it existed in books.

PS:
In 1969 the Pentagon introduced the ARPANET (after ARPA: Advanced Research Projects Agency), which through the 1970s and 1980s gradually evolved into the Internet…and then in the 1990s we had the World Wide Web.

LS:
And watching this evolution, so near yet so far from what might have been, must have been ungodly frustrating to Ted, like a wrong fork taken in what could have been the right road. Some of us watched similar just-not-the-same evolutions of what we had hoped would become the realizations of our own visions.

PS:
Project Xanadu is Ted Nelson's holy mission. It all began in 1960 with that computer course at Harvard. Vannevar Bush and the Internet came to function as practical triggers. However, over the years, as he discovered the work of some remarkable computer programmers and computer artists, Nelson broadened his vision.

LS:
Let's call it "Phase 2" then starting from 1960: trying to realize, to implement the vision. Funny things can happen to a vision on the way to Real Life. Things bog down in specifics, details, subprojects, tangential tasks, and a vision might not be communicable to one's tech-level collaborators in the first place, or might overlap with theirs but the implementation skews in the someone else's direction. The pros and cons of doing tech alone are that you are not constrained by anyone else's tendency to go a different direction or do interpret an idea another way, but what you create is limited by your own technical skills—a dilemma.

PS:
Ted Nelson's *Computer Lib/Dream Machines* had two front covers, no back cover. One front cover was for *Computer Lib*, which dealt with computer politics and tech. Flip the book over, start reading from the other cover and you have *Dream Machines*, dealing with the visionary use of computers. Stylistically *Computer Lib/Dream Machines* was modeled on Stewart Brand's *Whole Earth Catalog*, interspersed with hip illustrations, weaving odd stories and quotations into the text. The book was not meant to be read in a linear fashion. For 1974, it was completely revolutionary.

LS:

The forms Ted's early books took showed the essence of the problem. We simply don't think in sequential streams. Those early books of Ted's did their best to circumvent the limitations of words on paper. Their forms wanted to jump out into multiple dimensions. If he could have put hyperlinks between the ideas on different pages his books would have been too densely knotted up to be able to even open. Those books came closer to how the mind thinks, structurally, than any other books I can think of.

Xanadu was all about making non-sequential, non-hierarchical media a reality, a human common practice. As Ted put it himself in his book *Dream Machines*:

> Of course, if hypermedia aren't the greatest thing since the printing press, this whole project falls flat on its face. But it is hard for me to conceive that they will not be.

PS:

Then Tim Berners-Lee packaged the Internet for the masses, with Andreessen tossing in graphics. Years earlier Ted Nelson had intended to stretch the Internet's boundaries, as well as making it universally accessible. Sadly, HTML allowed Berners-Lee/Andreesen's web to spread like wildfire. Graphics and still images only enhanced websites' magazine feel. Instead of flipping through paper magazines, people pointed and clicked their way through ersatz electronic'zines. Ironically, audio/video capabilities furthered this paper ambiance. Since audio/video clips demand specific software (i.e., players), they are self-contained within their own virtual space (defined by these players) outside the virtual paper space (defined by HTML) of websites. Full screen video scarcely negates my point; in fact, it proves it. Over the web full screen video is either present or not: i.e., experienced in and of itself. Shockwave is no different: just animations embedded within their own software. Ted Nelson's version of the Internet was seamless, absolutely fluid.

LS:

The existing web as a set of containers for simulated pre-internet media. Yup.

PS:

Which brings us right back to James Joyce and Marcel Proust, authors whose writings swung toward multimedia…seamless multimedia; virtual reality…virtual reality not in the sense of Jaron Lanier, but Antonin Artaud.

Most people believe Jaron Lanier coined the term virtual reality in the early 1980s. Indeed, virtual reality is considered synonymous with the interface glove and head-mounted. But Artaud put those two words together – "virtual" and "reality" – back in the early 1930s. Artaud's virtual reality was a modern equivalent of alchemy.

Antonin Artaud (1896–1948) was a poet, surrealist, theatrical visionary. In the "The Alchemical Theater," Artaud wrote:

> All true alchemists know that the alchemical symbol is a mirage as the theater is a mirage. And this perpetual allusion to the materials and the principle of the theater found in almost all alchemical books should be understood as the expression of an identity (of which alchemists are extremely aware) existing between the world in which the characters, objects, images, and in a general way all that constitutes the *virtual reality* of the theater develops, and the purely fictitious and illusory world in which the symbols of alchemy are evolved.

Artaud envisioned alchemically charged multimedia environments physically enveloping, spiritually transforming audiences. In theater (as actor/director/writer/producer) he never came close to fulfilling his vision. This was partly due to a lifetime of drug abuse, but mostly because he was working in theater. Artistically Artaud longed for fluidity, seamlessness, a blurring not only between different mediums, but one that existed between artist and audience. Modern theater audiences were emotionally shut off from such shamanic possibilities. In the 1920s and 1930s film and radio were rigidly one-way mediums. Computers were in their most fledgling state and the Internet did not exist.

LS:

Ted and Artaud share that frustration of unrealized visions of new media fitting our mind's ability to experience.

It's amazing how much technological innovation has its inspiration in the arts, or in the human impulses that give rise to artistic expression. The literary and philosophical genesis of Ted's thoughts on informational structure are part of this aesthetic experiential innovation-motivating thread that runs through our species creations as a navigator piloting the unexplored technological spaces we are populating.

It makes additional sense in that both of Ted's parents were major figures—the director Ralph Nelson and the actress Celeste Holm—in the dramatic arts. He must have felt insignificant when he was young, with his famous parents getting so much attention. He outdid them though, creating, not repertoire in existing forms, but new informational structures with unprecedented aesthetic properties, whole new media to populate. We can now take for granted following stories with multiple endings, or choosing our own paths through narratives, poems that shuffle themselves into different shades of meaning, multi-stream multiscreen fiction with multitasking audience members each finding their own meanings, process pieces that once set in motion will continue to reveal additional evolutions, algorithmic music generators that never repeat... These kinds of meta-artistic creations point us toward new uninhabited potentials for expressing our experience the way the mind knows it subjectively, the way we think that we think we perceive. I guess this is sort of an ultimate case of "The medium is the message." Ted created new media initially because he needed them as an artistic being. Then instead of populating them with his own art, he made his life's work the struggle to give us as much freedom of structure as he could, so we can express, interconnect and begin to capture better the ways we experience thought in our minds. Or at least that was, I think, the vision before other people's ideas and interests pointed the Internet's evolution in the directions it took.

PS:

Marshall McLuhan, who, to the best of my knowledge, wasn't familiar with Artaud's theories, had this to say regarding computers in his 1964 book *Understanding Media: the Extensions of Man*:

> Our very word "grasp" or "apprehension" points to the process of getting at one thing through another, of handling and sensing many facets at a time through more than one sense at a time. It begins to be evident that "touch" is not skin but the interplay of the senses, and "keeping in touch" or "getting in touch" is a matter of a fruitful meeting of the senses, of

sight translated into sound and sound into movement, and taste and smell. The "common sense" was for many centuries held to be the peculiar human power of translating one kind of experience of one sense into all the senses, and presenting the result continuously as a unified image in the mind.

LS:
The ultimate interconnectedness would be shared consciousness, which the various arts tend to aim for, putting our individual expressions through the narrow bottlenecks of language, music, visual art and our species' other various mediating structures.

PS:
Ted Nelson wrote in *Computer Lib* (1974):

Everyone should have some brush with computer programming, just to see what it is and isn't. *What it is:* casting mystical spells in arcane terminology, whose exact details have exact ramifications. *What it isn't:* talking or typing to the computer in some way that requires intelligence by the machine. *What it is:* an intricate technical art. *What it isn't:* science.

LS:
He is right. Programming can be an art, although often it is hack work instead— just like in any other art.

TN:
For some reason people seem to think I don't understand computers simply because I don't buy into the prevailing paradigms—for example, the path name and hierarchical directories, which must be eliminated… We need a different world and how to built it is the question; not how do we take one more step toward the light because that's like trying to pile up chairs to reach the moon. It won't work.

LS:
Sort of like the mythological "IBM Man-Year": Instead of a programmer working for 365 days on a project, hire 365 programmers to work for just 1 day. But yes, hierarchy and other Aristotelian structures were helpful when data was scarce 2,000 years ago, but they don't fit what and how we experience the rich info ecology we now live in or the way our minds perceive.

PS:
Antonin Artaud sought the Holy Grail via alchemical theater, virtual reality. Artaud propounded magical realms transcending physicality. Computers can help us hone the physical world internally, reshape its virtual reality in cyberspace. Ted Nelson points toward interactive software synthesizing disparate media, breaking them down to their most basic form: in the case of text, a single letter; with graphics and still pictures, any part of an image; with audio, a lone sound, solitary intonation, or note of music; with video, a frame. Coded properly such software could generate a fierce hypermedia cascade reflecting the way words, images, and sounds rush through our minds. Wired globally, one might tap universal consciousness. Vaporware? For the moment, yes, but Project Xanadu is moving in the right direction with Ted's ZigZag as a first step. And since how future artists and information providers reap benefit from their wares must impact culturally every bit as much as style and content, Transpublishing, Ted Nelson's alternative approach to copyrighting, also brings us closer to the broader vision.

LS:

Yes, *ZigZag* is another of Ted's quite interesting innovations in informational structure. It puts the user in the place of a single point of consciousness that is able to move along any of many dimensions, moving associatively, by quality or characteristic instead of connecting stuff by symbolic reference or position in a hierarchy. I think it may well be much closer to how our human memories locate info within our own minds than the index tables or hierarchical nested directory structures or symbolic links we're so used to seeing info organized into.

ZigZag might also be a productive structure to create works of multisensory art within, as has been the cased already with hyperlinked text. ZigZag is more of an environment that the user inhabits. Depending on what someone builds into a ZigZag data space, you could wander along many multisensory paths, taking unexpected turns down the dimensions of color then branching off into textures or shapes, or from a sound to a flavor... Maybe multivoice music-like counterpoint could also be explored in the paths through ZigZag's spaces, with cognitive dissonance resolving to cognitive harmony—or whatever. I could see my *Music Mouse* software running around inside a ZigZag space.

Transpublishing and the way linking would have been done were Ted to have designed the Web, these deserve much more thought than they're getting. One of the great deficits of the existing public web, with its one way links is that there is no way to trace anything back to its origin, no provenance. It's as thought it's all forward-thinking, rootless.

PS:

I asked Ted about Vannevar Bush's essay "As We May Think."

TN:

I think I read it when it came out in 1945. Since I was eight, my memory is necessarily incomplete. Everyone else who would have been in the family is now deceased. But we did subscribe to the *Atlantic Monthly*, and I think there's a very good chance I read it at that time.

LS:

That might have been a bit of a mind-blow at age 8. Then again if the magazine lay around the house a few years, he could have read it when he was older. It's fun to think that that paper might have been the original non-standardizer for the way Ted's mind works.

PS:

Of course, he became thoroughly familiar with the essay later, printing it in its entirety in his book *Literary Machines*.

LS:

Lest we forget it, and/or because so few know it.

PS:

Then I asked him, "Were you more shaped by writers like James Joyce and Marcel Proust or by filmmakers like Sergei Eisenstein and Orson Welles?"

TN:

Both. I was an intense media kid. I remember my first movie experience was walking down the aisle of a theater in rural New Jersey and Shirley Temple singing on the screen. I just froze in my tracks. A goddess was singing to me.

**The moment included even the smell of the carpet and the Coca Cola. From
there, cinema was always my church. But then we read a lot at home, and
Shakespeare was essentially the god of the house. So between these different
media I never saw any conflict. To me, all media were one from the very
beginning.**

PS:

And I asked about Project Xanadu.

TN:

**I hated the idea of things becoming unavailable…and still do. Preservation,
access, unification are central. As soon as I saw in 1960 that media would all be
digital…well, then why have separate media anymore? It would all be one… to
me it's all hypermedia. We need to be able to create structures much richer
than there are now. Yet the notion of really blending these things is just as foreign to these guys today because they're so locked into the particulars of individual pieces of software and that's got to be stopped.**

LS:

Not only individual pieces of software but for many centuries before, individual
art forms, separate sensory modalities, human expressions hierarchically catego-
rized into specific art forms: text, art, music, and their subspecialties. The computer
is the Rosetta Stone for all the human arts. All media are representable within the
single digital domain, all structures and shapes within each of the arts being trans-
latable into all others and specifiable or editable with very similar tools and techniques. But the way software is being designed preserves the inherited separations
between them that unnecessarily compartmentalize our experience and keep expression and communication from becoming far closer to experience as we live it inside
of our individual minds. Béla Julecz back at Bell Labs called this the *Cyclopean
Retina*, the cognitive locus at which we humans experience all our diverse inputs as
one integrated perception.

PS:

In *Computer Lib*—remember, this was written in 1974, pre-Apple Computers,
pre-Microsoft, indeed, pre-Altair, which came out in 1975—Ted wrote:

A new era in computers is dawning. The first, or Classic, computer era used straightforward
equipment and worked on straightforward problems. The second, or Baroque, computer era
used intricate equipment for hard-to-understand purposes, tied together with the greatest
difficulty by computer professionals who couldn't or wouldn't explain very well what they
were doing.

But a change is coming. No one company or faction is bringing it about, although some
may feel it is not in their interest. I would like to call it here the DIAPHANOUS age of the
computer. By "diaphanous" I refer both to the transparent, understandable character of the
systems to come, and to the likelihood that computers will be showing us everything (*dia*-
across everything, *phainein*- to show).

In the first place, COMPUTERS WILL DISAPPEAR CONCEPTUALLY, will become
"transparent," in the sense of being parts of understandable wholes. Moreover, the "parts"
of a computer system will have CLEAR CONCEPTUAL MEANING. In other words,
COMPUTER SYSTEMS WILL BE UNDERSTANDABLE. Instead of things being complicated, they will become simple.

LS:

Not exactly what we've ended up with, with so many layers of hardware and software APIs interacting.

PS:

What does Ted Nelson think of the notion of a *diaphanous computer* today?

TN:

I've had my nose to a narrower grindstone.

PS:

Narrower…?

TN:

In the sense that what I'm trying to do is create portable data that is location-free. The web fetishized the hierarchical directory and path name, now called a website. This was completely evil. You wanted exactly the opposite: data that could be replicated without location and always recognized wherever it was. Turning my attention to that is one of the principle things I'm on now.

LS:

This is not to be confused with the *location-free* model that is now called *the cloud*. That's more like a return to the old architecture in which a large central computer would be accessed from many different terminals, except today's access devices are smarter and usually portable, such as iPhones.

Instead, what Ted appears to envision is more than portability in terms of access location. It includes, I suspect, that the way the data is structured can be different amongst the "locations" it is perceived from. This might be like a variety of filters on different cameras, but instead of filtering frequencies of light or of sound, the filters would be based on cognition-compatible structures, more like kinds of presentations, windows into different structures of perceptible space.

I think, but am not sure, that such a data space might be associatively structured, with links amongst common parameters, common values of parameters, possibly much like ZigZag's space, though Ted probably just means a single instance viewable from anywhere in many contexts via links.

PS:

I mention "The Death of the Author," Roland Barthes' essay advocating a neo-socialist Nirvana with free flowing information and no copyright laws.

TN:

Which, by the way, because of people's natural tendency to hoard information, for either political, strategic, or other reasons, is an unfortunately impossible dream. I see copyright as the one way creative individuals can get a leg up, no matter what the techies say. There was always a hidden agenda with them. "We'll just destroy it because it is manifest destiny that it be destroyed." I too want Nirvana, although not socialist, nor neo-socialist. My aim is figuring out rational principles of availability and access that are fair to all parties and legally workable. Techies put forth that since everything can be copied, therefore, we'll just destroy copyright. Today I'm dealing with a very brilliant, very rich techie who simply says, "I'll just buy a library, digitize it, and then the

publishers will have to deal with me." I'm saying we have to be a little more delicate about it.

LS:

It's a vision from the info consumer's side, not from the creator's. It ignores the investment of time, energy and thought into the creation of whatever's being accessed or copied. Still, there is a lot to be said for public domain ownership including "open source". It has to be the creator's decision of course, what level of ownership to respect.

PS:

Mark Harden's Art Archive has a vast array of beautiful scans. For all intents and purposes, it's a virtual storehouse of art treasures dating back to cave paintings. The site's philosophy is that people should feel free to lift five or six images for non-profit purposes. Yet does not reality dictate that anyone can lift as many images as they please and put them to whatever use?

TN:

There's two realities. At the Battle of Trafalgar, or some such battle, Admiral Nelson declares, "Full speed ahead!" His assistant protests. "But what about those ships?" Nelson, holding up a telescope to his blind eye, the eye everyone knows is blind, replies, "I see no ships." Or..."Do what I said." When you say "reality dictates," there are a lot of realities... So that is why I do not countenance most of today's so-called web standards... We need something much better and it is my duty to try to make a different reality which can supplant that other reality. I mean, a few hours on the web and you can have a whole lot of gifs and jpegs. Now, those things are being posted with a lot of implicit assumptions which the courts will be settling later, and whether you can repost, etcetera, is entirely uncertain... By the way, all these museums that are trying to claim copyright on 2000 year old things that they happen to own, God knows what's going to happen with that...like copyrighting the human gene.

PS:

Computer Lib decries "the creeping evil of Professionalism." "I see Professionalism as the spreading disease of the present-day world..."

TN:

I guess my claim at this point on that subject would be that everybody is seeking greater legitimacy and better pay for what they do, whether welding chips together, typing, or passing on the supposed validity of art objects. Professionalism is the stance that "I am highly trained; therefore, my work should be very expensive." In the case of what Talcott Parsons called professionalism, a highly technical definition, we have an association which governs entrance to the trade based on competence and training. So there's considerable similarity between the Plumbers' Union and the American Sociological Association. The upside is charlatans are pushed out of the field. The downside is talented but unqualified people are pushed out and you don't have all the options you should.

LS:

Nowhere is that professionalism elitist class more obviously breaking down than music. There used to be clear distinctions based largely on expertise: Do you read and write music notation? Do you play an instrument with great skill? Do you have a path to your audience through any of the established distribution bottlenecks (music publishers, radio stations, concert venues, record labels)? Computer technology has put those criteria into the past. Anyone can now create music, notation or instrumental skills being no longer required due to many new digital interfaces to sound. Anyone can netcast, podcast, stream, or publish music online. The line between *professional* and *amateur*, to the extent that it survives at all, is too blurry to be useful. And the same goes for visual art, writing, photography, cinema, leaving perhaps only the most physicality-mired creative professions relatively proficiency class based. This lack of a professional élite that can be clearly differentiated from non-professional creative workers is part of why the economies of the various arts are in such chaos due to computer tech.

Now the most stable economic value seems to reside more so in the tools used for creative work, marketed as intellectual property in themselves, instead of in what is made using them. But the design of tools for creative work is too often no longer being done by their users, and such tools often very much limit both creative conception and output. Too often they require a work to be highly preconceived in advance of even launching software to explore. Often they present a menu of templates for project types and standard formats within a medium, shunting their user into one a prefabricated standard form. And for Ted's main medium, words, we are still locked into sequential text editors in which it would have been impossible to write Ted's earlier books.

Laziness? Lack of imagination? Conservatism? Fear? Or a market-based, profit-based, tool-building industry that knows its bread is buttered by lowest common denominator non-thinking? Or maybe we are simply expecting things to change more radically, faster than they can, because while technology can speed up and get cheaper very quickly, other changes require profound paradigm shifts in the assumptions of entire social cultures.

TN:

I always wanted creative control of software and it's taken me till now to get it. I didn't realize that since the techies thought they could design interactive software no one in the world had any right to tell them otherwise. The decision process of Hollywood applies, a market system whereby people's claims to magic are centrally dealt with, so that some people are deemed to have magic, like Spielberg, because they reliably bring in money. That being the simplest and most easy to measure criterion of magic. Those who have a different kind of magic that doesn't bring in money, like Orson Welles, don't get the backing, and there's a whole big middle ground. I was definitely a disciple of Welles. When I was 15 I joined something called Cinema 16, a movie society. I attended a few of their screenings. What it really drove home to me was that you could make very inexpensive films, very personal films. I remember "L'Atalante" by Jean Vigo, a lovely low-budget French film about a canal boat people lived on. Then we had Norman McLaren's stuff. The Scottish animator just drew on film, drew on the soundtrack, creating short films with pens and pencils. His work was a great surprise to everyone. But it was also the fact that it was pack-

aged by the National Film Board of Canada. If they had not somehow given it their imprimatur I think no one would have given McLaren a chance. Still, I was impressed by how much you could do with very little. I was going to be a low-budget filmmaker, work my way up in Hollywood…until I saw a computer and that was my undoing.

People keep asking me how Xanadu is different from the web. It's like how is plankton different from the Queen Mary. There's just no resemblance. When it comes to preservation, access, writing—yes, writing itself, a horrendous problem just not understood by technical people—version management, rights management, reusing content and knowing you're reusing it, original context, regarding all these things the basic Xanadu model was entirely straightforward. Content would be registered, given final addresses, and we would distribute lists of content, essentially what are now called EDLs—Edit Decision Lists. Which is to say now put this here, put that there. Each piece of content would be paid for as you bought it from the rights holder, upon choosing it from the EDL. This is an extremely clean model. What I'm doing now is moving it forward into the web, trying to simplify it because in the 1988 Xanadu model we had it all gummed up with proprietary techniques. Ah, there we were in 1988, colossally efficient…and the web just threw out everything. Rights, management conversion, seeing context, seeing origins, unbreakable two-way links…forget it. They got it all wrong, but it can still be fixed. The courts are going to stomp in… The crackdown is coming and it's going to be so nasty, and they don't get it.

I'm just trying to create the rational system the web should have been in the first place and would have been if we hadn't screwed up politically. Tim Berners-Lee fashioned a way of pointing at conventional files and conventional directories via path names, visible to the user, over the Net. To me the notion of files and hierarchical directories is an unfortunate tradition that messes up the very nature of content. Marc Andreessen added Technicolor, all the special effects garbage he could cram in, glorifying, fetishizing these hierarchical directories which are now called websites and are located at URLs. So you have one-way, ever-breaking links, a shop window model, whereas you don't want to have to put it in a single place. That's like saying that such and such a book is the book you'll find on the fourth shelf, third from the right. It's ridiculous. The book should have a title and be retrievable from anywhere without the so-called URL. It's all about the politics of standardization. The political moves required…I hope I'll be able to make them. It's not websites themselves that are limited, but the keyhole through which you have to look. The main question is whether in this chowder that is the web we can create a new channel which is clean and clear and that's what I'm trying to do.

Chapter 7
Intertwingled Inspiration

Andrew Pam

Intertwingularity is the idea that everything is deeply interconnected on multiple levels. I will therefore describe my own background and experiences with Ted Nelson, comment on some issues raised by other contributors, and describe my views on the intertwingularity of modern popular culture.

I have always been interested in both technology and culture, and I attribute this partly to my background. One of my early recollections is that when I was very young and my mother was carrying me around in her arms I would actually reach out to light switches and flip the lights on and off. From the age of about three or four I was particularly fascinated by "exclusive or" light switches, where you have a room with the need for switches at two different doors and so they are wired up in such a way that both switches control the light and you can turn it on or off from either door. As a child I then went on to explore in sequence: electricity, electronics, digital electronics and early computers. We had ancient computers at my school. We had a PDP-8 and then an LSI-11 and an Apple II and so on up through the history of computers. I was interested in each level of hardware: how the physics of transistors worked, how digital circuits were put together, and how CPUs operated. When I was young, I designed a simple CPU and a simple operating system. I asked my brother to sit underneath a desk, fed him instructions, and had him execute them.

In parallel with that interest, I have also always been interested in culture, both national cultures and popular culture. My grandfather was an Austrian Jewish industrialist who was murdered by the Nazis, and there is a commemorative plaque for him in Vienna. My grandmother was part of the Bohemian movement and fled to Australia via England, where my father was born. My mother is a musician, and my father is a very educated and cultured gentleman who founded and conducts the Melbourne Musicians orchestra. We always had a lot of books in our house, and as a young boy I read *The Complete Sherlock Holmes*, *The Complete Lewis Carroll*,

A. Pam (✉)
Project Xanadu, 138 Lincoln Rd., 3136 Croydon, VIC, Australia
e-mail: xanni@xanadu.net

© The Author(s) 2015
D.R. Dechow, D.C. Struppa (eds.), *Intertwingled*, History of Computing,
DOI 10.1007/978-3-319-16925-5_7

Shakespeare, Arthurian legends, and so on. I was encouraged to read and became quite a rapid reader. At school I read the entire school library. I started with the things that most interested me like fantasy and Science Fiction, and then I worked my way though all the fiction until ultimately I'd read all the detective fiction, all the romance novels, and everything else as well. Sometimes I'd go through ten books a day! In the process of reading through the school library, I was very fortunate because they happened to have a copy of *Computer Lib/Dream Machines*. That was my first exposure to Ted and his ideas.

This was about 30 years ago, around 1984. I was still in high school, I was sixteen at that time, and I immediately wrote off to Project Xanadu, which I believe was sponsored by Autodesk at that point. Ted's book included an invitation to get involved in the project, and he responded by sending me some documentation. I continued to receive periodic postal updates from the Xanadu Project for the next few years. I even got an early Xandle, a *Xanadu Handle* intended to be a permanent unique network identifier. A few years later I met my lovely wife Katherine Phelps who is a writer. She was born and raised in the United States and got her BA and MA degrees there. She then completed her doctorate in creative writing for digital media in Australia after we married. I introduced her to Ted and his work that she found just as fascinating as I did. When we took a trip to visit her relatives in the US, we contacted Ted and Marlene and asked whether we could meet them while we were there. We stayed with them on their houseboat and hit it off immediately.

Katherine and I subsequently organised a speaking tour for Ted in Australia. I became Ted's system administrator and have run his Xanadu servers including email and websites since 1994. I've also had the pleasure of assisting in various other ways. I did an early text-based prototype of Zigzag, and we did some experimentation with very early belt mounted Pentium III wearable computers. They radiated considerable heat into your body! More recently I was delighted to participate in Ted Nelson Month at the Internet Archive.

I'm an avid collector, and Katherine and I collect all kinds of media. We've always needed to have a house big enough to accommodate a library. We have a computer game collection, a book collection, a comic book collection, and a video collection. Professionally I've been a computer programmer and a system administrator, and I have always had an interest in computer-mediated communications. Computers are now central to the way we communicate. Katherine and I used to run one computer bulletin board. It grew into a three-state network of bulletin boards, and we got involved in the Internet. I was involved in implementing connections between the early Internet and teletext technologies very early in my career. Over the years I've spent a lot of my spare time either following along relatively passively or actively participating in Ted's work. Thanks to Kay Nishi, I've had the joy of working with Ted in Japan for a while, and I hope to continue collaborating with Ted for some time to come. There's still plenty more to do!

I find that one of the reasons an event like this can be productive and inspirational is because it allows people not only to discuss each other's work, but also to talk about other interesting connections and see how they might relate to their own ideas. I was delighted to see the little video from Frode Hegland's students because it's certainly true that Ted's work has continuously appealed to new generations, and each new generation has found something to like about and connect with in Ted's work. It's often said that you don't really want to try and do Shakespeare scholarship because there's so much Shakespeare scholarship already that you're reduced to finding the tiniest little niche to do a doctorate. With Ted's work, there is so much yet to do because he has taken on such a grand challenge. There's so much opportunity for people to leap in and join in the project.

During the conference, there was some discussion about books as an operating system. A prominent use of that concept is by the British novelist Jasper Fforde in his *Thursday Next* novels. Fforde explicitly features the idea of a book operating system as a device within the novels. Additionally, many of the characters are aware that they're fictional characters moving between different levels of reality into and out of different fictional worlds. He also applies the concept to the print books themselves. On his website he asks his readers to apply patches and to write in the frontispiece of the book what version of the book they currently have after they've fixed errors in the book as originally published.

I also have a story about simulations. A school was using simulations as a teaching aid. They had some software that allowed students to simulate running their country. There was a 10-year timespan in the game. One group of students realised that they could apply a bit of meta-game thinking. Because the simulation was going to end after the 10th year, they could pretend the world did not exist in the 11th year, and they could just completely loot the treasury and do all kinds of things that took advantage of this discontinuity. This is unexpectedly realistic emergent behaviour. It is analogous to what politicians often do when they know they can't be re-elected due to term limits. I like this story because it shows that the assumptions encoded in the design of a simulation do often reveal quite a lot in and of themselves.

I also wanted to respond to Noah Wardrip-Fruin's comments about games with shooting as a primary mechanic.[1] I've long been interested in computer games as a medium—they're fun and good way to learn. It is of course very well known that many computer games are about shooting. One of the reasons for this I think, as some game critics have said, is that it's partly because when you're looking at ways to interact with a virtual world, destruction is one of the first and most obvious ways to have an effect on the world. It's kind of a 2 year old's way of dealing with the world: poke at things and see if they break! A big check-box for game designers was "can we add more destructibility to the environment." Thankfully, we're now starting to move beyond that and explore other things that games can do.

Finally, one of my great passions is the intertwingularity of popular culture. I'm very interested in what is usually referred to as "fan fiction." Fan fiction isn't really a separate thing from other fiction and never has been. Published authors sometimes play in other authors' worlds. For example, Neil Gaiman wrote and published an H. P. Lovecraft spoof called *Shoggoth's Old Peculiar* and contributed a story called

---

[1] See in this volume, Noah Wardrip-Fruin, Chap. 14: *We Can and Must Understand Computers NOW*.

A Study in Emerald to an anthology combining the worlds of Arthur Conan Doyle and H. P. Lovecraft. Many authors have written Sherlock Holmes stories, including Lois McMaster Bujold. She wrote a story called *Adventures of the Lady on the Embankment*. The story features a protagonist called Cordelia Naismith. The character would later became the genesis of the initial protagonist of the same name in Bujold's series, the *Vorkosigan Saga*. John Scalzi, a noted Science Fiction author and recent president of the Science Fiction Writers of America, wrote his own reimagining of an H. Beam Piper novel which he (Scalzi) wasn't originally intending to publish. His agent liked it and contacted the Piper estate to obtain permission to publish it.

There have been a number of "shared worlds" in the past where authors or publishers chose to invite multiple authors to write within the same fictional universe, and Amazon is trialling a system where authors can grant permission in advance for other people to write within their worlds. In Japan, the animation studio Gainax famously started out as a bunch of fans who eventually became professionals. There's always a conversation between the audience and the creators. To some extent we're all both consumers and creators of culture. This has always been the case, but the Internet has acted as a force multiplier for this just as it has for many other things. Ted's ideas for structuring the "docuverse" are still very much needed to provide more powerful ways to see the connections and the context of the relationships between works.

I've recently become interested in the 2010 relaunch of the 1980s children's TV franchise *My Little Pony*, not only because Katherine and I are animation fans and as has been discussed by numerous media articles and three separate documentaries so far it has surprisingly broad appeal well beyond the core demographic of young girls but also because it is dense with references and has become a particularly good example of this kind of culture as a group activity. *My Little Pony* has a sequence which is intentionally a shot-for-shot remake of a scene from *Star Wars* and a recurring character based on Q from *Star Trek* and voiced by the same actor, John de Lancie, who constantly makes references to shows like *Harry Potter* and *Mary Poppins*. The franchise has also frequently incorporated ideas originating with the fans. This kind of interaction with other works is considered post-modern, but it's also made very visible something that's always existed: that culture is really one big intertwingled thing.

Of course many other fandoms have become popular enough to support significant creative communities, for example *Harry Potter* fandom has spawned "Wizard Rock" as a musical genre. But toy company Hasbro, the owners of the rights to *My Little Pony*, have been unexpectedly willing to tolerate and even support the fan activity. Much to their credit, they have realised the opportunity to benefit from the fan works and have on many occasions chosen to permit the use of their trademarks rather than use them heavy-handedly to ban fan works. A company called "We Love Fine" produces and sells a wide range of T-shirts with *My Little Pony* fan art that requires both copyright permission from the fan creators of the art and trademark permission from Hasbro. Hasbro have also begun licensing the creators of 3D models based on their characters to sell 3D prints of those models, starting with *My*

Little Pony and planning to expand to their other toy franchises such as *Transformers*. This is very forward looking because 3D printing may soon come to have a significant impact on the toy market.

These kinds of interconnections between cultural works, and between the creators and the fans, are great examples of the increasingly prominent intertwingularity of the modern world. I hope that Ted's Xanadu ideas will continue to inspire the tools we all use to navigate this ever more interwingled Internet world and will enable people to more easily create interconnected works and discover and communicate the connections between them. I look forward to discovering what the next 30 years will bring and as Ted says, "onward and umpward!"

Chapter 8
An Advanced Book for Beginners

How *Computer Lib/Dream Machines* Shaped Our Perspective on Cybercrud, Interactivity, Complex Texts and Computer Creativity

Dick Heiser

8.1 Introduction

Computer Lib/Dream Machines [1] arrived in 1974, exactly in time for the personal computer revolution. It was privately printed and published by Hugo's Book Service. He kept the inventory in his garage.

At The Computer Store, people wanted to find a way to get up to speed quickly about personal computing, but there hadn't been time for mass media to develop a perspective. Enter *Computer Lib/Dream Machines*. We enjoyed recommending it to everybody. The book's enormous size and two-sided format let people know reading it was going to be an interesting adventure. Over our first several years, we sold hundreds of copies. When Microsoft re-issued the book years later, it's clear they tried to civilize it, but everything they tried seemed to backfire. The giant pages resisted being squeezed into a smaller format, and the radical changes Ted Nelson predicted in 1974 were already starting to come about.

Computer Lib/Dream Machines is one of the best examples of a technically advanced book delivering a powerful vision of personal empowerment and enlightenment. It set the tone for the personal computer revolution!

8.2 Cybercrud

We forget how bad the old times were. People were told to do things a certain way "because that's the way the computer requires." Ted was the loudest voice calling out this mistake. He called this thinking *cybercrud*, and *Computer Lib/Dream*

D. Heiser (✉)
Los Angeles, CA 90045, USA
e-mail: dick.heiser@gmail.com

© The Author(s) 2015   51
D.R. Dechow, D.C. Struppa (eds.), *Intertwingled*, History of Computing,
DOI 10.1007/978-3-319-16925-5_8

Machines was about empowering users to demand computer systems that accommodate humans rather than the other way around.

Ted pointed out that video games don't have error messages; games just do something reasonable and proceed. The digital dashboard in your car does the same. We have also awakened to the unnecessary annoyance of too many dialog boxes: "Are you sure you want to quit?"

For example, a programmer might phrase a telephone call message: "Illegal number; call aborted!" The telephone company did a better job: "We're sorry, your call cannot be completed as dialed; please check the number and dial again."

We've made such substantial progress in this sphere that we don't have to think about it much anymore. We can look to the Macintosh, iPhone, game console, auto dashboard and Siri for good examples of how to interact with a machine. On the Internet, Amazon, Google, Facebook and Bank of America operate outstanding websites that are flexible, capable and a pleasure to use. This is huge. There are still bad websites and bad software, some of it spectacularly bad, but the example of the good ones will drive out the bad ones.

8.3   Interactivity

David Albrecht of People's Computer Company (PCC: what a radical name!) discovered and promoted *Computer Lib*. People's Computer Company operated a timesharing BASIC computer lab in Menlo Park, and published a newsletter on interactive computing. The newsletter told me how to get the book. PCC also published a big book of computer games in BASIC, called *What to Do After You Hit Return*. One guessing game was called "Hunt the Wumpus." It was lucky for Ted that Bob Albrecht knew about *Computer Lib*, because Hugo's Book Service had few contacts among computer enthusiasts.

Ted also chose only interactive interpreted languages to explain programming: TRAC, APL and BASIC. This is an amazing and powerful way to give a perspective about programming. Ted also discussed the importance of simulation and graphics, of course.

8.4   The Hands-On Imperative

One of the biggest changes has been in the way we see computers. In the 1960s computers stood on raised flooring behind locked doors and you needed an account number, meaning a serious business purpose, to participate. In fact, if you weren't a big organization dealing with lots of money, you'd be told to forget using computers anyway. Computers were for math rather than for literature or connecting with others or discovering ideas. Ted's book awakened people to a bigger vision.

The personal computer revolution was a very emphatic experience for those of us who considered ourselves activists; we knew hands-on computing was a big deal and we felt the pushback from the computer industry establishment. We called it a revolution and it really was one.

People's Computer Company was way ahead of its time. It featured the "hands-on imperative." Starting in 1975, user groups in Los Angeles and the Bay Area educated people and helped them find answers and resources. Byte Magazine was started; conventions, swap meets and newsletters spread the word. Everybody can participate. We have layers of powerful, responsive, computing resources from handheld to the cloud.

8.5   Complex Texts

Rectangular tables of data are not the only way to organize information in a computer. Lyall Morril developed *Whatsit?* a freeform information organizer that used triples to record relationships between entities. That was a little step toward loosening up people's thinking in the direction Ted was and is advocating.

I am especially grateful to Ted for introducing me to Douglas Engelbart, another amazing visionary, the man who gave "the mother of all demos." Engelbart showed creative ways of organizing work and ideas, and of collaborating online.

An attorney customer of ours created a program to organize legal arguments. His program let a user connect evidence to arguments and arguments to evidence. Primitive personal computer languages made it difficult to store text strings longer than 256 characters, but even with those limitations, the program worked well.

8.6   "Everything Is Deeply Intertwingled"

The quotation that serves as the heading for this section appeared on page D2 in the *Dream Machines* half of Ted's book, *Computer Lib/Dream Machines* [1]. Ted was key to the development of hypertext, but he's disappointed that we didn't make links that work in both directions. Even one-way links can be amazing. I had a transformative experience with a Hypercard program called *The Dungeon of Class Gifts*. It trained lawyers about the rules for group inheritance. It's very light-hearted and breezy. After each page of explanation, you're asked a question with two possible answers. If you choose the right answer, you advance to the next screen. Choose the wrong one, and you're sent to a screen picturing an explosion. The screen says "a mind is a terrible thing to waste" and then the computer sends you back to the beginning of the lesson. Gradually you progress farther into the sequence. By the time you're nearly done, you have answered the first questions many times, and you are energized; you're in a hurry to finish the lesson. It's basically a game of Parcheesi!

The game forces you to rehearse the facts enough times to learn them. It's a delightful way to be seduced into memorizing something!

8.7 Xanadu

It was fun to hang out with the Xanadoodlers, especially in the 1970s and 1980s. Xanadu is a daring design that presented awesome challenges: how to link to evolving documents, how to track changes to a document, how to manipulate linkages, how to organize archival storage, how to name the target of a link, how to track micro-copyright royalties, how to organize the physical storage of a universe of discourse and how to scale storage and processing around the world.

Many people are still skeptical of the need for bi-directional links. I am one who suspects links might only occasionally need to be bi-directional, or that a pair of one-way links could simulate a bi-directional link.

Claude Shannon's popular demonstration of his computer-controlled maze-navigating mouse was essential to the success of his project. Shannon's demonstration appeared as a segment in the television show, *Time Machine: Robots* [2]. Shannon went to a lot of trouble to prepare a tabletop maze and to eliminate any arm or cord connecting the mouse to the computer. This greatly enhanced the impact of his presentation, and of his theory. It helped Shannon gain traction with his audience.

Similarly, Xanadu needed terrific examples of information organized with Xanadu using bi-directional links, examples of change tracking, annotation and link navigation. This would have helped less-abstract thinkers like me understand the system better. Showing how to write a response to a 100-page Request For Proposal would give Xanadu a chance to show off.

Many problems still perplex even fans of Xanadu. I can't imagine how to organize the millions of links that might want to connect to popular texts like the Bible or the U.S. Constitution.

It was a constant struggle to try to implement Xanadu on the computers available at the time. Hardware was way too expensive, too small and too slow. Nowadays, we could prototype the system with JPEG screenshots. Google's massive datacenter technology would be just the ticket for running Xanadu.

8.8 Computer Creativity

We had a poster in our computer store quoting Ted about the creative possibilities inherent in interactive computing. I re-read *Computer Lib* looking for this quote, and found many surprises, including the *Computer Lib* pledge (Fig. 8.1). I also found where I learned many of my basic perspectives about computers.

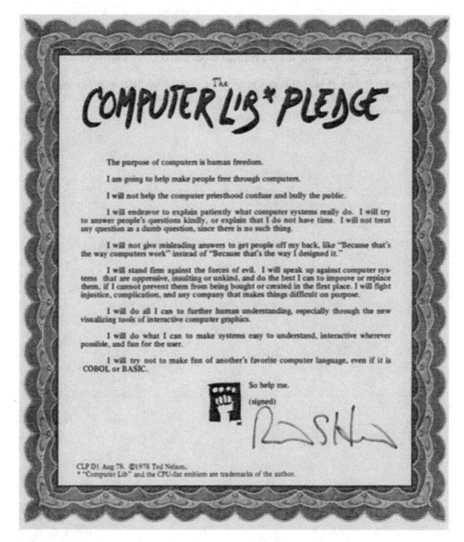

The purpose of computers is human freedom.

I am going to help make people free through computers.

I will not help the computer priesthood confuse and bully the public.

I will endeavor to explain patiently what computer systems really do. I will try to answer people's questions kindly, or explain that I do not have time. I will not treat any question as a dumb question, since there is no such thing.

I will not give misleading answers to get people off my back, like "Because that's the way computers work" instead of "Because that's the way I designed it."

I will stand firm against the forces of evil. I will speak up against computer systems that are oppressive, insulting or unkind, and do the best I can to improve or replace them, if I cannot prevent them from being bought or created in the first place. I will fight injustice, complication, and any company that makes things difficult on purpose.

I will do all I can to further human understanding, especially through the new visualizing tools of interactive computer graphics.

I will do what I can to make systems easy to understand, interactive wherever possible, and fun for the user.

I will try not to make fun of another's favorite computer language, even if it is COBOL or BASIC.

So help me.

(signed)

Fig. 8.1 The *Computer Lib* pledge

Computer Lib was just the right advice for someone shopping for a personal computer in 1975! It's an advanced book for beginners!

References

1. Nelson TH (1974) Computer lib: you can and must understand computers now/dream Machines. Hugo's Book Service, Chicago
2. Time Machine: Robots. *Robots*. History Channel. Aug.–Sept. 2000. Television. See segment on Claude, Shannon. 1952. *Theseus Maze-Solving Mouse*. (begins at 9:16 in the video). http://youtu.be/KmURvu4x0Do

Part III
Hypertext and Ted Nelson-Influenced Research

Chapter 9
The Importance of Ted's Vision

Belinda Barnet

Sometimes a journey makes itself necessary, as Anne Carson puts it in *Autobiography of Red* [3, p. 46]. For Nelson it has been a long journey, at times a very difficult one, but it has been necessary. Necessary for him personally—as he puts it in *Possiplex*, "I have no alternative but to go on. Like Shackleton of Antarctica I find myself enmeshed in a harsh duty that was not the original plan... I will fight for it to my last breath" [10, p. 339]. He has survived the journey so far, his ideals held high above the mud. But as the *Intertwingled* conference has demonstrated, as the people who have spoken here have demonstrated, the journey has also been necessary for the computing world.

Nelson's vision is, I think, the most important vision in the history of computing. That's a tall call, so I'll need to explain my reasoning. In my book *Memory Machines* [1], I argue that the *idea* of a universal digital publishing system, an "open hypermedia" system, originated with Nelson. Bush's vision, though it was about connected items, was analogue. Engelbart's vision was also profoundly important. He was first to build many of the things we take for granted in modern computing (and I don't mean the mouse; I mean the whole concept of real-time, networked, interactive computing). His contributions would take hours to elaborate. But he was not thinking about hypertext as a domestic thing–something your mom and pop would consume over latte and a cheeseburger. Nelson saw that hypertext on a computer screen would spread around the globe like electronic kudzu vine. He wrote singing commercials for it; he even sketched a quirky interior for a Xanadu café.

What Nelson saw was an anarchic, global hypertext publishing system: a "digital repository scheme for world-wide electronic publishing" [9, p. 3/2]. While working at

B. Barnet (✉)
Media and Communications, Faculty of Health, Arts and Design, School of Arts,
Social Sciences and Humanities, Department of Media and Communication,
Swinburne University of Technology, Hawthorn, Australia
e-mail: BBarnet@groupwise.swin.edu.au

© The Author(s) 2015   59
D.R. Dechow, D.C. Struppa (eds.), *Intertwingled*, History of Computing,
DOI 10.1007/978-3-319-16925-5_9

Harcourt in 1966 he dubbed the project Xanadu. Although he was not the first to build it, he predicted that hypertext would have *domestic penetration* before anyone else.

Nelson had a rich vision for what Xanadu should look like and the experience it should deliver to the public. The design went through many iterations, which are best explained in *Literary Machines*. They varied in their details, but all contained intercomparison or the re-use of elements (later dubbed transclusion) in some form. I'll talk about how these ideas evolved briefly here.

The vision started in 1960, and Nelson tends to get cranky at me when I begin in 1965 because that is the first published record (historians like bits of paper published at the time in addition to human memory). The designs, he told me in 2011, 'had been swirling in my head for 5 years' before then (Nelson 2011, pers. comm.). I will be starting in 1960 today, but I want to stress that this is based on Nelson's recollections in *Literary Machines,* on his autobiography *Possiplex,* and on our personal interviews. I'd love to go through Nelson's archives and find a term paper or file card from 1961. Nelson has shown me tantalizing video footage of a box of file cards from the 1960s. That's like watching porno for a media historian.

According to *Literary Machines* (and his autobiography), Nelson did a term writing project for the IBM 7090 in 1960. The IBM, the only computer at Harvard at the time, was stored in a big, air-conditioned room at the Smithsonian Observatory [9, p. 1/25]. That setup would have cost over two million dollars back then, and it wouldn't have had a screen.

Nelson believes he saw a screen in a manual at one point – as he told me in an email a couple of weeks ago, "I remember it very clearly. A round CRT and a flat desk surface, a light pen" (Nelson 2014, pers. comm.). This was apparently not Ivan Sutherland's Sketchpad, which was built in 1963, and Nelson has been unable to find the image again in the IBM 7090 manual). In *Possiplex*, he writes:

A few words, a few pictures of people at computer screens, and the understanding that computer prices would fall—these gave me all I needed to know, a crystal seed from which to conjure a whole universe [10, p. 100].

In 1960 Nelson proposed a machine-language program to store documents in the computer, change them on a screen with various editorial operations, and print them out. This was no mere word processor, which in any case didn't exist at the time; Nelson envisioned the user would be able to *visually compare* alternative and prior versions of the same document on-screen. That's an important strand of Nelson's thinking that would continue on, comparing documents in parallel, or "intercomparison."

Intercomparison was a radical idea to dream up in 1960, when computers were for serious people (like engineers) to solve serious problems. At that time people were computing with cards. A "terminal" was a teletypewriter, used by an "operator", who put in the cards and tore off the printouts. In the mid 1960s you could, if you were rich enough, acquire a "glass teletype", a video-type display that acted like a teletype, but I don't think that would have been available in 1960.

Back then computers were million-dollar things that demanded refrigeration and respect. You "talked" to them with punch cards and got your answer on a printout. Nelson conjured a different universe from a crystal seed. Fourteen years later, in

Computer Lib, he would write, "if computers are the wave of the future, displays are the surfboards" [8, p. 22].

The second part of Nelson's vision took shape in the early 1960s, when there was "a lot of talk around Cambridge about Computer-Assisted Instruction, for which there was a lot of money" according to *Literary Machines* [9, p. 1/26]. At this point, Nelson's project was not so much a design, he stressed when I asked for records once again (I must annoy him with my desire for bits of paper), he said, "it was an idea that may have been on only one file card" (Nelson 2011).

At this stage he devised what he called "the thousand theories program," an explorable computer-assisted instruction program that would allow the user to study different subjects by taking different trajectories through a network of information. In *Literary Machines* he writes, "This idea rather quickly became what I would eventually call hypertext" [9, p. 1/26]. He thought of the system as incorporating many separate, modularized paragraphs, each with branching choices: writing as a graph, not a single line or sequence.

This led to another idea, which Nelson drafted as an academic paper while teaching sociology at Vassar College in 1965. That would become the transclusive relationship—and eventually ZigZag. It also got him published for the first time, which is why historians like to use that date.

In his 1965 paper for the ACM, "A File Structure for the Complex, the Changing and the Indeterminate" [5], Nelson proposed a display-based computer system that permitted linking between documents and the re-use of elements called Zippered Lists. Again, this was at a time when the whole idea of text on a screen was seen as a waste of processing power, let alone bizarre "nonsequential" text.

In 1965, unless you were working on Doug Engelbart's team or could afford a system with video-type display (Nelson reasons it "would cost less than a secretary" in his paper, at $37,000 in 1965 money, which would be a well-paid secretary), computers were expensive things with more important jobs to do. For most organisations they *still* didn't have screens.

I should also stress that, in 1965, text was not data—it was something academics and journalists manipulated with typewriters. As Doug Engelbart told me in 1999, the whole concept of a human being sitting in an interactive feedback loop with a computer, manipulating symbols on a screen, was foreign to most people in the 1960s.

It was wacky even in the seventies, when we had it working–real hypermedia, real group-ware working. (Engelbart 1999, personal communication)

As some eminent speakers discussed during the conference, this was a "paradigm problem" Nelson would later take on in *Computer Lib*. In fact, he did more than just take it on. He declared outright war on the established computer religion—particularly the idea that computers belong to a rarified priesthood. So although that declaration was best made with a raised fist (and capital letters) in *Computer Lib*, it had been brewing for him since 1960.

For the time being, in 1965, he ignored the dominant paradigm and published his zippered list design. That paper, when you think about what a computer was meant to be used for at the time, had chutzpah. He called the design the "Evolutionary List File" or ELF.

In this system, items in one sequence could become part of another like the teeth in a zipper—except the two sides of the zipper didn't have to be in the same order. Versions of a document could be visually intercompared, and all items could be written or retrieved in a nonsequential fashion. Links could be made between large sections, small sections or single paragraphs. Most importantly, however, chronological stages and sections in a document could be retrieved and compared. You could trace the evolution of an idea.

In his autobiography, Nelson reflects that the ELF design was "strange and hard to understand. In fact, it was quite bad" [10, p. 151]. It did, however, include facilities to compare versions of a document and reuse elements from these versions. Both of these ideas would make their way into Xanadu in some form, but the zippered list in particular would eventuate in a "deliverable" 30 years later: ZigZag.

In that same 1965 paper, Nelson claimed that computers would eventually "do the dirty work of personal file and text handling" [5, p. 85]. Needless to say, personal computing has happened. The dirty work is now done by clunky programs like Microsoft Word—programs Nelson has a go at every now and then.

Not because he's a cranky "'one-note-samba' fellow who can't find another idea to push" and "should have moved on by now" as one programmer put in on a *Lambda the Ultimate* blog post (this programmer may not be happy that I'm including him here—[14]), but because the computing world could be completely different. That's always been his message, even in the 1960s.

In 1967, having seen Engelbart's NLS, Nelson went on to predict a networked structure of information that would "be read from an illuminated screen; the cathode-ray display; it will respond or branch upon actions by the user. It will be a succession of displays that come and go according to his actions" [6, p. 195]. That succession of displays that respond and branch has also happened. It's hard to imagine a world without it, actually.

The idea that the Xanadu system should be an open or shared access publishing system, what this talk is really about, also started in the 1960s. Although in 1967 he envisioned a sort of "super Executive's Console," which was self-contained. He writes in *Literary Machines* that in 1967 "the idea of communicating between such consoles was beginning to get through to me, and the nagging issue of shared access began to grow on me" [9, p. 1/31].

It may have been growing on Nelson in 1967, but as I've said, the computing world really wasn't about to swallow the idea of a global hypertext publishing system. Work had not even started on the ARPANET (though Ivan Sutherland and Bob Taylor had been thinking about it for some time). The computing establishment was still trying to grapple with the concept of a person sitting in front of a screen and exploring information in real-time after Doug's mother of all demos in 1968. That demo took years—over 20 years—to filter through properly.

There was, however, an attempt to build part of Nelson's vision at Brown University in 1967, and that resulted in a unique and historically important standalone system called the Hypertext Editing System. I'm not going to go into that here, however—this is Nelson's party and I don't want to poop it. If you are interested you can find it in my book [1], and the implementation notes are published in the Xuarchives [7]. I'll just say that it didn't happen the way he wanted it to happen.

Nelson had also met Engelbart and seen his landmark NLS system by 1967. The friendship would last until Engelbart's recent death. (Although Nelson had initially thought this meeting happened in 1967, he found some notes while writing *Possiplex* and realized it was in 1966. Those notes have since been lost!)

He thought Engelbart was warm and wonderful upon first meeting him, though he did not like the "hierarchical" structure of Engelbart's system. He went on to dedicate his book on Xanadu, *Literary Machines*, to this "visionary of The Augmentation of Human Intellect…and (what this book is largely about) THE TEXT LINK" ([9]—"1987 Dedication" included in 1993 edition).

Nelson and Engelbart were close: they understood each other on multiple levels. In his passionate eulogy for his friend, Nelson said, "I don't just feel like I've lost my best friend. I feel like I've lost my best planet" [11]. Although their visions were different, they shared some similar life experiences. Firstly, Engelbart and Nelson watched their ideas spread around the globe then re-emerge as someone else's interpretation, an *approximation* of a vision. That has upsides and downsides.

I remember putting it to Nelson once, in Melbourne, when he was getting a bit despondent about his life, that he has "inspired" people. He told me immediately that this was never his intention, and that the problem with inspiring people is that they then try to credit you with things you don't like (Nelson 2011, personal communication). He never set out to "inspire" people: he wanted to create an entirely new computer world. He wanted to actually build that world, not watch other versions of emerge. The fact that it has not yet been built drives him to continue.

Englebart and Nelson also lived through resistance: resistance to those original visions in the 1960s. I don't want to dwell on this, but I think it does need to be said. There have not always been conferences like this one held in Nelson's—or Engelbart's—honour.

Although Engelbart, as an engineer with a prestigious post at SRI, had more basis for conversation with the computing mainstream, what he was doing was not seen as "science" back then either. As the Head of Engineering at SRI told a young Bill Duvall (and Duvall later recounted to me), "You don't really think what they're doing up there is science, do you?" (Duvall 2011, personal communication).

That kind of resistance has dogged Nelson for many years. People didn't understand what he was going on about, and neither Ted nor his vision seemed to fit in any one nice explanatory box. As *The Economist* put it in 1986, "Boon or boondoggle, nobody is quite sure" (cited in [9], preface). Discussion of Xanadu still positions his work in left field.

As others have discussed, in 1974, in *Computer Lib*, he took his idea to the public, in the hope that he may have better luck there. He argued that computers are mere changeable devices for twiddling symbols that should power this new all-singing, all-dancing media experience for everyone. It was a rallying cry to that cause. Some of the conference attendees were actually around when that book was published, and they have unpacked its importance for personal computing. I just want to talk about hypertext.

One of the main things I want to emphasise is that for many years it was up to Nelson to promote the idea of a world-wide hypertext publishing system. It may be self-evident, even pedestrian today, but it certainly wasn't in the 1960s and 1970s— right into the 1980s people were still building workstation-based hypertext systems.

HyperCard, the elephant in the pre-Web hypertext room that introduced the concept of linking to the general public, was a stand-alone system. NoteCards, Guide, etc., none of these were globe-spanning open publishing systems. Even in the 1980s, it seemed wacky.

In a 1988 paper given at Oxford that Nelson provided to the participants of this conference (I hadn't seen it before) called "Hypertext: the Manifest Destiny of Literature" Nelson writes, hopeful as ever:

> The key problem is…to create a universal literary medium, an unbounded storage and delivery system as simple in concept as the book and library, unrestricted as to what screens you may see it on, unrestricted in its organization, unimpeachable in its authenticity, and as quickly available as a phone call. (Nelson 1988)

So it wasn't obvious even then, either, in 1988. It wasn't obvious that it was needed and that it was about to happen on a massive scale.

It was not until the Web that people really saw and understood, as Jay Bolter put it in our interview, that "the really interesting things happen when your links can cross from one computer to another," from one continent to another (Bolter, Jay David, Interview with the author, 2011). Then it all became rather obvious.

Nelson had been arguing for a global hypertext for a long time before the web. The thing is, he was not the first to build it, and that must have been deeply frustrating (particularly when they built it WRONG, he would add).

The Web is not Xanadu. It just looks a lot like what he'd been talking about all that time. It is also, crucially, what hypertext looks like to at least two billion people around the world. But Nelson won't "move on" and find "another idea to push" because he can see that it could be so much better.

In 1999, Nelson told me:

> The web is a universal, world-wide, anarchic publishing system. It completely vindicated my 35 years of saying that a universal, worldwide, anarchic publishing system would be of enormous human benefit. There is no question of whether it is of benefit. It just does it all wrong, that's all (Nelson 1999, pers. comm.).

Somewhere around 1993 Nelson found he no longer had to convince people that such a network was possible; you just had to switch on your machine to see that it was. His task changed to convincing people that Xanadu would be better. I should add here, if it isn't obvious by now, that I believe him.

But I've learnt some things from studying the history of hypertext. The first is that hypertext is not the Web. The Web is but one implementation of hypertext. People had been building and designing hypertext systems decades before the web arrived, and many of them did things the web just doesn't do. Xanadu in particular still has much to offer us. The Web is great in that it actually works, for most people, most of the time—and it has stayed the course for 25 years. It is not, however, the only way hypertext can be done.

So back to the title of my talk: the importance of a guiding vision.

The remarkable thing about Xanadu is that, despite countless setbacks, it refuses to die. Its logo is, appropriately enough, the Eternal Flaming X. Paisley and Butler (cited in [12, p. 262]) have noted that "scientists and technologists are guided by 'images of potentiality'—the untested theories, unanswered questions and unbuilt devices that they view as their agenda for 5 years, 10 years, and longer." Often accused of hand waving and lucid dreaming, Nelson's Xanadu has nonetheless become inherited vision.

But engineering discourse has always privileged prototypes over ideas – things that are concrete. Working prototypes, working algorithms, real deliverables that you can see in action. The same might be said for computing science. As Vincent Childress put it, the "main criteria applied to engineered technological solutions is that they work" [4], or more precisely, that they are seen to work.

For this reason, I think, people have been able to write off the Xanadu design as a pipe dream, particularly Gary Wolf in his scathing Wired article [13]. But the thing about the process of invention and innovation is that vision and prototype work in unison; they work together. Without an image of potentiality – the untested theory, the unbuilt device, the unanswered questions – innovation becomes a process of stabbing around in the dark.

You have to pick your vision, and your visionary, carefully though. You would want that vision to solve a problem that you think people are facing, for example (incidentally the reason why Engelbart had "flashes" of himself sitting at a Memex-like machine while driving home in 1950, a flash that changed the world). You would want that visionary to be right, at least some of the time, about what the future might hold. You would also want it to be technically feasible. And by that I mean, extrapolating from the devices, technologies and ways of doing things available to me right now, can I build it one day? Most importantly, you would also want it to be guiding you somewhere beneficial.

On that note, I'll leave the last piece of my talk to Engelbart. As Nelson put it in his eulogy, "No one ever had such a soaring view of human potential as Douglas Carl Engelbart—and he gave us wings to soar with him, though his mind flew on ahead, where few could see" (2013).

This is an excerpt from the 1995 Vannevar Bush Symposium. Engelbart was on the stage with Nelson, Alan Kay and Tim Berners-Lee. A member of the audience (referred to in the transcript as "Bob Franston"—this was probably Bob Frankston, co-creator of VisiCalc) asks a question of the panel, that starts with:

> I'm not going to defend Windows, but what I want to try and understand is why Windows is such a problem. If you have to change the world all at once and you can't coexist with what exists, you've got a problem…. Do you really feel like you have to change all the world at once?

Engelbart, who had in fact already changed the world by that point, though not all at once, answered him.

The only thing I can say is that you have to pilot software, there has to be some sort of conscious pursuit of that future that you can't really guarantee is there, but [you need to] look... (Vannevar Bush Symposium [2]).

We have to consciously pursue a future that is beneficial; we have to pilot ourselves towards it; we have to look. There is no other way. I think that is what Ted has been doing since 1960.

References

1. Barnet B (2013) Memory machines: the evolution of hypertext. Anthem Press, London
2. Brown University/MIT Vannevar Bush Symposium (1995) Notes from the panels. http://cs.brown.edu/memex/Bush_Symposium_Panels.html
3. Carson A (1999) Autobiography of red: a novel in verse. Vintage Books, Random House, New York
4. Childress V (1998) Engineering problem solving for mathematics, science, and technology education. J Technol Educ 10(1). http://scholar.lib.vt.edu/ejournals/JTE/v10n1/childress.html
5. Nelson TH (1965) A file structure for the complex, the changing and the indeterminate. In: Proceedings of the ACM 20th national conference. ACM Press, New York, pp 84–100
6. Nelson TH (1967) Getting it out of our system. In: Schlechter G (ed) Information retrieval: a critical review. Thompson Books, Washington, DC, pp 191–210
7. Nelson TH (1968) Hypertext implementation notes, 6–10 March 1968. Xuarchives. http://xanadu.com/REF%20XUarchive%20SET%2003.11.06/hin68.tif
8. Nelson TH (1974) Computer lib: you can and must understand computers now/dream machines. Hugo's Book Service, Chicago
9. Nelson TH (1993) Literary machines. Mindful Press, Sausalito
10. Nelson TH (2010) Possiplex: movies, intellect, creative control, my computer life and the fight for civilization. n.p., available at Lulu: http://www.lulu.com/shop/ted-nelson/possiplex/paperback/product-14925222.html
11. Nelson TH (2013) Eulogy for Douglas Engelbart. Speech at Technology legend: honoring Douglas Engelbart, computer history museum, mountain view California, December 9th 2013. http://www.youtube.com/watch?v=FNCCkhADpiw
12. Smith LC (1991) Memex as an image of potentiality revisited. In: Nyce J, Kahn P (eds) From memex to hypertext: vannevar bush and the mind's machine. Academic, London, pp 261–286
13. Wolf G (1995) The curse of Xanadu. Wired 3(6). http://www.wired.com/wired/archive/3.06/xanadu.html
14. xeo_at_thermopylae (2004) Comment on a Lambda the ultimate blog post at Wed, 2004-09-01 18:52 http://lambda-the-ultimate.org/node/233#comment-1729

Chapter 10
Data, Metadata, and Ted

Christine L. Borgman

10.1 Introduction

My conversations with Ted Nelson began in earnest in 2004 when we shared an office at the Oxford Internet Institute (OII). He was working on Xanadu, and I was working on *Scholarship in the Digital Age: Information, Infrastructure, and the Internet* [7]. My work was in conversation with Ted's since I was a graduate student, having read *Computer Lib* early on. Ted signed my copy of *Literary Machines* [25] at a talk in the mid-1990s, thus I was in awe of the man when Bill Dutton put us together as visiting scholars in the OII attic, a wonderful space overlooking the Ashmolean Museum.

Ted and I arrived at concepts of data and metadata from very different paths. He brought his schooling in the theater and literary theory to the pioneer days of personal computing. I brought my schooling in mathematics, information retrieval, documentation, libraries, and communication to the study of scholarship. While Ted was sketching personal computers to revolutionize written communication [24], I was learning how to pry data out of card catalogs and move them into the first generation of online catalogs [6]. Our discussions that began 30 years later revealed the interaction of these threads, which have since converged.

C.L. Borgman (✉)
Department of Information Studies, University of California, Los Angeles, CA, USA
e-mail: borgman@gseis.ucla.edu

© The Author(s) 2015   67
D.R. Dechow, D.C. Struppa (eds.), *Intertwingled*, History of Computing,
DOI 10.1007/978-3-319-16925-5_10

10.2   Collecting and Organizing Data

Ted overwhelms himself in data, hence he needs metadata to manage his collections. He drapes himself in data collection devices (Fig. 10.1). On any given day, he carries some combination of paper notebooks, a packet of colored marker pens draped on a string over his shoulder, a video camera, still camera, audio recorder, and other recording devices.

Ted's data immersion is not simply about recording one's life experiences, as in Gordon Bell's MyLifeBits project [5]. Rather, Ted's data collection encompasses information relevant to documentation, writing, networks, and hypertext – anything that could possibly inform the design of Xanadu and related technologies. The common thread of the data collection projects of Ted Nelson and Gordon Bell is that both acquire heterogeneous data types that must be integrated. Bell, a distinguished computer scientist at Microsoft, has the resources to build a testbed for studying and exploiting those data (Gemmell et al. [15]). Ted, for whom necessity is the mother of invention, takes a much more informal approach to capturing, describing, and integrating the content he gathers. One of our first conversations was about metadata – he asked me to explain it, and as I started to do so, he asked me to stop and wait a moment. He pulled an audiocassette recorder from his jacket pocket, turned it on, said "Christine Borgman on metadata." Then he turned to me and said, "now talk about metadata" … and we did! At the end of that conversation, he made an entry in his daily diary about the conversation and where it was located on which cassette. Thus, Ted created a document (the recording), assigned a subject heading ("metadata") and a personal name entry ("Christine Borgman") as metadata about

Fig. 10.1 Ted Nelson, 2005, carrying data collection devices at the Oxford Internet Institute (Photo by Christine L. Borgman)

the document, and created a catalog record (the entry in his notebook). In this case his action was recursive, as he created a metadata record about metadata.

10.2.1   Theoretical Traditions

Formally, metadata is "structured information that describes, explains, locates, or otherwise makes it easier to retrieve, use, or manage an information resource" [23]. The NISO definition breaks metadata into the three general categories of descriptive, structural, and administrative. Other definitions of metadata make finer distinctions among types [2, 17].

Ted developed a fundamental understanding of data, metadata, and documentation through his work on hypertext and literary machines, despite his lack of familiarity with the field of information studies. He recognized that documents do not stand alone, even if they look like independent objects. Rather, they are deeply connected to many other objects. These relationships can be abstract, as in the influence of one text on the meaning of another – known as "intertextuality" in semiotics and literary studies. Relationships also can be explicit, when one document cites another, includes portions of other documents ("transclusions"), or makes any other direct link. These explicit relationships are the basis for hypertext and hypermedia, terms coined by Ted in the 1960s. The body of relationships among documents is sometimes known as "hypertextuality."

In documentation, usually dated to the Belgian, Paul Otlet, in the early twentieth century, texts are deconstructed into component parts and linked together. In the information sciences, Otlet's work is considered to be the precursor to hypertext [29–31]. Building upon the complex history of bibliography, documentation, identity, and philosophy of information, modern cataloging rules link together nodes of documents, authors, publishers, and other entities as a network [35]. The model known as FRBR, for Functional Requirements for Bibliographic Records, establishes four levels of entities: work, expression, manifestation, and item [36]. The *work* is the distinct intellectual creation, such as Shakespeare's play *King Lear*. The *expression* is the specific form, such as the text of the play as published in Shakespeare's First Folio. The *manifestation* is a physical embodiment of an expression, such as the Royal Shakespeare Company's 2007 production of King Lear in Stratford-upon-Avon starring Ian McKellen. The *item* is a single exemplar and a concrete entity, such as a specific copy of the program for a performance of that 2007 production. FRBR also establishes relationships among persons, corporate bodies, concepts, objects, events, and places.

10.2.2   Practical Consequences

Metadata, such as the familiar entities in a catalog record—author, title, publisher, date, place, physical description, subject, and classification—are essential descriptions of documents and other entities. Without metadata, a library would be no more than rooms full of books and documents shorn of their title pages. Metadata describes, enables access, and provides links to other documents. Some forms of metadata creation can be automated, such as extracting keywords and citations from a text, and others are created by human experts, such as descriptions of the intellectual content and history of an object.

Having stumbled upon the concept of metadata in our conversations, Ted was an eager student of knowledge organization. I introduced him to Ann O'Brien of the Department of Information Science at Loughborough University, one of Britain's experts on knowledge organization [20, 37]. Dr. O'Brien specialized in multi-media documentation, a particular challenge for Xanadu. While she was at first daunted by Ted's style of inquiry (Fig. 10.2), they quickly became able sparring partners. Ted, Ann, and I explored many aspects of metadata that might be applied in Xanadu.

Among the challenges that Ted encountered, long known to Ann and other experts in knowledge organization, is that the apparatus necessary to represent relationships between documents can be very large. Data, including texts, can be the tip of the iceberg. The metadata required to manage, to find, and to follow relationships amongst documents is often much more voluminous than the documents themselves. Furthermore, as networks grow in size, they become more complex, requiring other layers of representation and more sophisticated tools for navigation. Ted's concept of hypertext supports multi-directional links between documents (Fig. 10.3). His approach is aligned with semiotics, philosophy, and information science thinking about relationships between works [14]. However, multi-directional links are complex to implement computationally, which was especially true in the early days of personal computing. Technical compromises made in the early days of the World Wide Web undermined Ted's ability to implement hypertext on a large scale. He

Fig. 10.2 Ted Nelson and Ann O'Brien, Oxford, 2006 (Photo by Christine L. Borgman)

Fig. 10.3 Ordinary hypertext, with multi-directional links. From *Literary Machines* (Used with permission)

"ORDINARY" HYPERTEXT

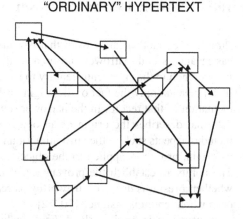

continues to rail at this constraint. Forty years after Computer Lib, computers are far more sophisticated and the networks among digital objects are much richer and more complex. It is time to revisit fundamental assumptions of networked computing, such as the directionality of links, a point made by multiple speakers at the symposium—Wendy Hall, Jaron Lanier, Steve Wozniak, and Rob Akcsyn amongst them.[1]

10.2.3   Managing Research Data

Managing research data is similarly a problem of defining and maintaining relationships amongst multi-media objects. Research data do not stand alone. They are complex objects that can be understood only in relation to their context, which often includes software, protocols, documentation, and other entities scattered over time and space [8]. The need to model these complex relationships stimulated technical research in persistence, identity, and linking of research objects [4, 26, 28, 38]. These approaches build upon—and are limited by—the technical capabilities of the World Wide Web.

As research data become valued as objects to be maintained, reused, and repurposed, many stakeholders are coming together to address questions of linking, identity, and stewardship. These concerns cross boundaries of scholarly communication, computer science, publishing, research funding, libraries, archives, data repositories, and education [8, 9, 13, 34]. Breakthroughs on these data problems may contribute to understanding hypertextuality, and vice versa.

---

[1] See in this volume Wendy Hall, Chap. 11: *Making Links: Everything Really is Deeply Intertwingled* and Rob Akcsyn, Chap. 15: *The Future of Transclusion*.

10.3   Provenance and Pluralism

Provenance, another fancy word that was unfamiliar to Ted but basic to his ideas, has meanings both narrower and broader than *metadata.* The term was borrowed from French in the eighteenth century to indicate the origin or source of something. It can mean simply the fact of the origin or the history of something and the documentation of that record. In the narrower sense, provenance can be a type of metadata that describes the origin of an object. Provenance on the World Wide Web includes aspects such as the attribution of an object, who takes responsibility for it, its origin, processes applied to the object over time, and version control [16, 21]. The ability to establish the provenance of a dataset, for example, may influence whether a result is deemed trustworthy, is reproducible, is admissible as evidence, or to whom credit is assigned [10, 22].

Provenance is particularly difficult in hypertext because it requires not only establishing authoritative links between objects, but also sustaining those links and information about the links over long periods of time. These links remain reliable only if the identity of the object can be established uniquely at the item level [1, 32, 33]. Unique and persistent identifiers need an institutional home, whether an International Standard Book Number, which is maintained by national libraries [19]; a Digital Object Identifier (DOI), which is maintained by the DOI Foundation and stored in interconnected registries ("Digital Object Identifier System" [11]); an Open Researcher and Contributor Identifier (ORCID) for author names, which is maintained by a non-profit foundation and stored in interconnected registries [18]; or domain-specific identifiers, such as those for genomics, chemistry, and so on. Lighter weight solutions, such as Linked Open Data, can be used to establish rich sets of relationships among objects, but these are not intended for long-term stability [3, 27]. In scholarship and in research data, stable linking is essential to follow chains of evidence. The apparatus to establish and to maintain those links cannot exist in a vacuum. Rather, it is part of a larger knowledge infrastructure, one that is now being imagined anew [8, 12].

Ted's notion of "pluralism" is that "anyone may revise anything – harmlessly" ([25], 2/61). Pluralism expresses today's notion of use and reuse of digital objects. The social movement toward open access is predicated on the ability to borrow and reuse content, with attribution to the original source. Authors and other creators are more willing to share their works openly if they can expect credit for that work. Both credit and harmlessness thus depend on provenance. The original object must stay intact and later references to those originals must be sustained.

10.4   Conclusion

Ted has tackled—head on—some of the thorniest known problems of information organization. He lacked the background in the information sciences to know how hard these problems were. Yet hard problems often are solved by those who approach unaware of the littered path of failure. Ted brought fresh ideas to knowledge organization and stimulated those inside the field to revisit fundamental premises. The challenges that have stymied Ted are those that frustrated many who came before. Ted, like Paul Otlet, tried to develop a pure new system that did not depend on the technologies and bureaucracies of the day. Reinventing infrastructure is even harder than reinventing literature, and he has tried to do both. Ted has a large following in the library world because he dared to reimagine the library. Everything is indeed intertwingled, another provocative term of Ted's invention. Xanadu, the hypertext system, is related to Samuel Taylor Coleridge's 1797 poem about the summer palace of Kublai Khan, is related to the Yuan dynasty, is related to the ruins of Shangdu in Inner Mongolia, is related to … the many other paths of inquiry to be pursued in the ideal world of comprehensively networked knowledge.

References

1. Agosti M, Ferr N (2007) A formal model of annotations of digital content. ACM Trans Inf Syst 26(1). doi:10.1145/1292591.1292594
2. Baca M (1998) Introduction to metadata: pathways to digital information. Getty Information Institute, Los Angeles
3. Bechhofer S, Buchan I, De Roure D, Missier P, Ainsworth J, Bhagat J, Goble C et al (2013) Why linked data is not enough for scientists. Futur Gener Comput Syst 29(2). Special section: Recent advances in e-Science: 599–611. doi:10.1016/j.future.2011.08.004
4. Bechhofer S, De Roure D, Gamble M, Goble C, Buchan I (2010) Research objects: towards exchange and reuse of digital knowledge. Nat Proc. doi:10.1038/npre.2010.4626.1
5. Bell G (2001) A personal digital store. Commun ACM 44(1):86–91. doi:10.1145/357489.357513
6. Borgman CL (1977) Library automation at Dallas Public Library. In: Shepherd CA (ed) Information management in the 1980's: proceedings of the ASIS annual meeting, Chicago, vol 40. Knowledge Industry Publications for American Society for Information Science, White Plains, p 29 (2–A9–A–14 Microfilm)
7. Borgman CL (2007) Scholarship in the digital age: information, infrastructure, and the internet. MIT Press, Cambridge
8. Borgman CL (2015) Big data, little data, no data: scholarship in the networked world. MIT Press, Cambridge
9. Bourne PE, Clark T, Dale R, de Waard A, Hovy EH, Shotton D (eds) (2011) Force 11 manifesto: improving future research communication and e-Scholarship. Retrieved from http://www.force11.org/white_paper
10. Buneman P, Khanna S, Tan WC (2001) Why and where: a characterization of data provenance. Lect Notes Comput Sci 1973:316–330
11. Digital Object Identifier System (2009) Retrieved from http://www.doi.org
12. Edwards PN, Jackson SJ, Chalmers MK, Bowker GC, Borgman CL, Ribes D, Calvert S et al (2013) Knowledge infrastructures: intellectual frameworks and research challenges. University of Michigan, Ann Arbor. Retrieved from http://deepblue.lib.umich.edu/handle/2027.42/97552
13. Force11 (2015) Home page. Force11: the future of research communications and scholarship. https://www.force11.org/about

14. Furner J (2010) Philosophy and information studies. Annu Rev Inf Sci Technol 44(1):159–200. doi:10.1002/aris.2010.1440440111
15. Gemmell J, Gordon B, Lueder R (2006) MyLifeBits: personal database for everything. Commun ACM 89:88–95. doi:10.1145/1107458.1107460
16. Gil Y, Cheney J, Groth P, Hartig O, Miles S, Moreau L, Pinheiro da Silva P (2010) Provenance XG Final Report. W3C Incubator Group. http://www.w3.org/2005/Incubator/prov/XGR-prov-20101214/
17. Greenberg J, White HC, Carrier S, Scherle R (2009) A metadata best practice for a scientific data respository. J Libr Metadata 9(3/4):194–212
18. Haak LL, Baker D, Ginther DK, Gordon GJ, Probus MA, Kannankutty N, Weinberg BA (2012) Standards and infrastructure for innovation data exchange. Science 338(6104):196–197. doi:10.1126/science.1221840
19. International Standard Book Number (ISBN) Agency (2013) Home page. http://www.isbn.org
20. Ma Y, O'Brien A, Clegg W (2007) Digital library education: some international course structure comparisons. Joint Conf Digit Libr 490. doi:10.1145/1255175.1255289
21. Moreau L (2010) The foundations for provenance on the web. Found Trends Web Sci 2(2/3):99–241. doi:10.1561/1800000010
22. Moreau L, Groth P, Miles S, Vazquez-Salceda J, Ibbotson J, Sheng J, Varga L et al (2008) The provenance of electronic data. Commun ACM 51(4):52–58. doi:10.1145/1330311.1330323
23. National Information Standards Organization (2004) Understanding metadata. NISO Press, Bethesda
24. Nelson TH (1974) Computer lib: you can and must understand computers now/dream machines. Hugo's Book Service, Chicago
25. Nelson TH (1994) Literary machines, 93rd edn. Mindful Press, Swarthmore
26. Object Reuse and Exchange (2014) http://www.openarchives.org/ore/
27. Parsons MA, Fox PA (2013) Is data publication the right metaphor? Data Sci J 12:WDS32–WDS46. doi:10.2481/dsj.WDS-042
28. Pepe A, Mayernik M, Borgman CL, Van de Sompel H (2010) From artifacts to aggregations: modeling scientific life cycles on the semantic web. J Am Soc Inf Sci Technol 61(3):567–582. doi:10.1002/asi.21263
29. Rayward WB (1991) The case of Paul Otlet, pioneer of information science, internationalist, visionary: reflections on biography. J Librariansh Inf Sci 23:135–145
30. Rayward WB (1994) Visions of Xanadu—Paul Otlet (1868–1944) and hypertext. J Am Soc Inf Sci 45:235–250
31. Rayward WB, Buckland MK (1992) Paul Otlet and the prehistory of hypertext. Proc ASIS Annu Meet 29:324–324
32. Renear AH, Dubin D (2003) Towards identity conditions for digital documents. In: Proceedings of the 2003 international conference on Dublin core and metadata applications: supporting communities of discourse and practice. Dublin Core Metadata Initiative, Seattle, WA
33. Renear AH, Palmer CL (2009) Strategic reading, ontologies, and the future of scientific publishing. Science 325:828–832. doi:10.1126/science.1157784
34. Research Data Alliance (2015) Home page. https://rd-alliance.org/node
35. Svenonius E (2000) The intellectual foundation of information organization. MIT Press, Cambridge
36. Tillett BB (2004) What is FRBR?: a conceptual model for the bibliographic universe. http://www.loc.gov/cds/FRBR.html
37. Tinker AJ, Pollitt AS, O'Brien A (1999) The Dewey decimal classification and the transition from physical to electronic knowledge organisation. Knowl Org 26(2):80–96
38. Van de Sompel H, Sanderson R, Klein M, Nelson ML, Haslhofer B, Warner S, Lagoze C (2012) A perspective on resource synchronization. D-Lib Mag 18(9/10):1–6. doi:10.1045/september2012-vandesompel

Chapter 11
Making Links: Everything Really Is Deeply Intertwingled

A Talk for Ted

Wendy Hall

Ted, this is for you. I've flown in for this event from Hong Kong. If I become incoherent it's because there's a 15-h time difference. I'm flying to London tonight because I have to be back for the weekend, so I can't stay for the dinner, but I wanted to be here for you. I only have 30-min and I've got a lot to say, in fact, I've got about 30 years of stuff to say. It is a great honor to be here. Thank you very much for inviting me. I really wanted to honor Ted, and support this wonderful event.

Throughout my life I have always tried to make links. When I got my chair at Southampton my inaugural lecture was entitled, "Making Links." It was about the hypermedia work we were doing at Southampton, but I'm also a social linker and I've always tried to link the different research communities, such as hypermedia, multimedia, the Web, the Semantic Web and others, to try to be a bit of glue in there that gets everybody talking together. Over my life I've found that everything really is deeply "intertwingled" and I'm very proud to say that this is my first Ted Talk. Well, it depends how you parse that. I first heard "TED Talk" in 1989, but I'm calling this *my* first Ted Talk. Now I'm going to tell you about me because I reckon if I do that Ted can't say I'm wrong. He could of course challenge the references to how he has inspired my life but I'll let him do that.

This talk is based on a standard talk that I give, but intertwingled with how Ted has inspired my career and my work, and my life generally. We were both inspired by Vannevar Bush's paper "As We May Think" [2]. Ted read it long before I did of course. I first read it in about 1987. I started my career as a pure mathematician—my PhD topic was algebraic topology—but in the Eighties I became increasingly interested in the application of personal computers in education. I got very, very interested in what we would now call multimedia. Do you remember the old twelve-inch analog video discs? I got really excited about how you could put a video on a computer and then teach people using this new interactive media.

W. Hall (✉)
Web Science Institute, University of Southampton, Southampton, UK
e-mail: wh@ecs.soton.ac.uk

D.R. Dechow, D.C. Struppa (eds.), *Intertwingled*, History of Computing,
DOI 10.1007/978-3-319-16925-5_11

As the new personal computers emerged onto the scene, I gradually moved more and more into computing. I went back to the University of Southampton in 1984 as a member of the computer science faculty, which surprised everybody including me because I loved pure mathematics. But the rest, as they say, is history because that move opened so many doors for me. So around 1986/1987, as I was beginning to find my feet as junior member of faculty, I started working in this new exciting area of multimedia.

In 1987 when I read Vannevar Bush's paper I also began to hear about this 'new' idea called hypertext. I began to hear about Ted and Doug Engelbart, both of whom equally inspired me: Ted talking about everything being deeply intertwingled, and Doug, talking about augmenting the human intellect. Again, I don't need to tell this audience about these two men. When I give talks to a non-expert audience I always include reference to them because it was their ideas—I hadn't met them at this point—that inspired me. The year of 1987 was a key one for hypertext. It was the year of the first ACM Hypertext conference, and the year Apple released HyperCard. It was also the year that the archive of the Earl Mountbatten of Burma arrived at the University of Southampton. Mountbatten was a cousin of the Queen, and very famous in the UK for his various military leadership roles during and after the Second World War and as the last Viceroy of India. What does this have to do with my research story?

The Mountbatten family estate is just outside Southampton, and after he died in the 1970s, the University of Southampton took over custodianship of his archive, which consisted of about 250,000 papers, 50,000 photos, audio recordings of his speeches and various film and video recordings. This was multimedia as it was in 1987. It was pre-digital library. Nothing was born digital then, we had to go through the process of digitizing it before we could view it on a computer let alone over a network. I thought how marvelous it would be if we could digitize all this material and use this new hypertext/hypermedia idea to make it available to anybody who wanted to find out what was in the archive without having to come to Southampton. We could link it all up! And we could, maybe, have different links for different people, so that if school children wanted to find out about something that was in the archive they would get different links to historians who were looking for evidence of what had happened when and why.

As I was mulling these ideas over, I was lucky enough to have a 6 month sabbatical at the University of Michigan in Ann Arbor in 1989, and this is when I first heard Ted talk at a Computers in the Humanities conference in Toronto. He was the keynote speaker. I was spellbound. I bought a copy of his book Literary Machines [5], and he signed it for me. We didn't really get talking at that conference but the book became my hypertext bible. I taught from it. I learned about hypertext and Ted's definition of the link and everything about Xanadu, tumblers, transclusions, micropayments and much, much more. They were all such exciting ideas, so much ahead of their time. Ideas that the world still hasn't fully appreciated, solving problems that the world is only just beginning to realize it has.

I came back from that sabbatical year really fired up about what we could do with digital archives and what was then becoming called the digital library. At Southampton we built a hypermedia system called Microcosm using the Mountbatten archive as our first demonstrator [3]. I wanted the system to be able to automatically create links on keywords in the application such as linking the names of key characters mentioned in the Mountbatten archives to their biographies or to a photograph. We called these generic links and they became a significant feature of Microcosm. Ted said we should have called them something other than links, as a generic link didn't fit his definition of a hypertext link, but by the time Ted saw Microcosm it was too late to change the naming of the links. Microcosm was an open hypermedia system in that all the links were stored in a database as first-class entities that could be reasoned about and applied to any document. Each link was a triple that consisted of a source, a destination and a description. Little did I know at the time how prescient of the Semantic Web these ideas would be. Of course, there are problems with automatically making a link on a word without knowing its precise semantic meaning. There are a lot of different people with the name Mountbatten in the Mountbatten archive for example. So working out the context in which the link was being applied and therefore the meaning of the word became a key focus of our work: problems we are still dealing with as the Semantic Web develops today.

We did also have specific links in Microcosm that were more like standard hypertext links because they were embedded in the documents and represented to the user through highlighted buttons, and you could trace them backwards though the link database or linkbase as we called it. But the really novel idea was the generic links that were stored in a separable hyper-structure and created on the fly.

We had the concept of a viewer in Microcosm, which you might call a browser today. We had a control system, which is where we went wrong because everything was centralized around that control system, even though the system itself could be distributed. And when the user said, "I want to see what links we've got on this word," then the query would be run through the control system and through a set of filters which determined the list of links that came back to the user through the link dispatcher. I had a lot of post-graduate students developing both the main system and experimenting with different types of filters. It was a great plug and play system for experimental research. There were a lot of ideas in this system that you now see working at scale in the Web and in the Semantic Web.

Remember we were doing all this using personal computer workstations and videodisc players. It all seems very primitive now when you think about the way we use the Web on our mobile phones, but the ideas ran deep. We developed tools to generate links based on the metadata description of documents, and if you do that the *docuverse*, to use Ted's term, just falls out. The pure mathematician in me just loved making these patterns. We also generated links on the *data* in the documents and using that idea we able to integrate (make links between) different types of documents: text documents, multimedia documents, spreadsheets, databases, etc.. We created links in picture, video, and audio files, and we did lots of experiments using the data to create links in multimedia archives. It was all very exciting and very prescient of the work we are doing in the Semantic Web and the world of big data today. I'm very proud to say that and not at all bitter when today's researchers don't make the links back to previous work. I just think how privileged we were to be able pioneer these ideas in the research lab and what fun it was.

Meanwhile, of course, at CERN in Switzerland, Tim Berners-Lee was thinking his own great thoughts that were going to change everything. It was 1989 when he wrote his paper "Information Management: a Proposal" for his boss at CERN in which he defined what would become the World Wide Web. At the time, it was quite complicated to download a document from the Internet. Most people used FTP. There were emerging systems such as Gopher and WAIS that were providing easier inter-faces and that had elements of hypertext functionality but were not that easy to use or readily available. In Tim's paper you see all the elements that he had distilled from the hypertext community, the generalized mark-up community, and the net-work community. It was those three ideas that came together in his design for a global hypertext system. His main aim was to enable anybody, but in particular physicists, to share information over this new thing called the Internet, basically at the click of a button. Tim's boss, Mike Sendall, marked his proposal as "Vague, but exciting" and this gave Tim permission to carry on developing his ideas as part of his day job.

I first met Tim at the European Hypertext Conference in Paris in December 1990. Our first paper on Microcosm was accepted at the conference [3]. Tim was there with his colleague from CERN, Robert Cailliau, talking about the system they were building that they hadn't yet called the World Wide Web. The list of attendees at the conference is available on the Web now so you can see who was there.

In 1991, the ACM Hypertext conference was in San Antonio in Texas. Tim had created the first website over the Christmas holidays in 1990, and he christened the system the World Wide Web. It was my first trip to Texas, one of my first trips to the States for work. This was the conference that famously rejected Tim and Robert's paper on the World Wide Web. Our second paper on Microcosm also ended up on the reject pile for this conference. What you do when you have a paper rejected from a conference is you submit a poster or a demonstration so you can still go to the conference. I was still junior faculty at the time remember. So we were in San Antonio demoing the Microcosm system, and Tim and Robert were demoing the World Wide Web. This was the first time I saw them demo it. I remem-ber looking over Tim's shoulder and thinking, "There's nothing new here. This hypertext system is hardly hypertext." In those early days, I used to set my students an essay with the title, "Is the Web hypertext?" because according to all the defini-tions at the time it wasn't. And I remember thinking "he embeds his links in the documents and they only go one way!" I mean, this was just so primitive. It wasn't going to go anywhere. And I wasn't the only person thinking that at the time. How wrong we all were.

I also remember thinking how pretentious to call it the World Wide Web. How was he going to persuade the whole world to use this rather primitive system? Well, he did. It has become the hypertext system that the whole world uses to exchange information on the Internet. Tim understood that the network was everything, and he recognized the need for the system to be distributed, decentralized and open, with universal standards to enable it to scale. He got the fact that scruffy works, in other words he allowed for human frailty by allowing for the links to fail. He also gave it away so there was no economic barrier to people using it. I think that's what really made the difference to the uptake. The problem we now have of course is that nobody owns the system that has subsequently been created, but that's another whole story.

We must also give credit of course to Marc Andreessen and his team at NCSA for their development of the Mosaic browser for the Web in 1993, which made it much easier for people to access the Web. At ACM Hypertext'93, half the demos were Web-based, and the first Web conference was in May 1994. We were still developing Microcosm as a research system, and we produced a commercial version in 1994, which did very well for a while. The company we set up raised over £13 million pounds of investment funding and is still in existence today, but by the end of the 1990s my research group was almost entirely focused on Web-based developments and much of the interesting hypermedia work encapsulated within the Microcosm project had to be shelved until the Semantic Web was mature enough to become an alternative development platforms. But of course, like others we were riding the wave of a truly World Wide Web which was changing society in ways it would have been hard to imagine just 10 years previously.

It was during this transition period at IEEE Multimedia 1996 in Hiroshima that Ted started to become interested in the Microcosm project. Two of our PhD students—Stuart Goose and Jonathan Dale—presented a paper about Microcosm at the conference and spent time talking about our ideas there with Ted [4]. They invited Ted back to Southampton to talk more and meet the rest of the team including me. I remember sitting with Ted and Marlene in the staff bar at the University just talking and talking. We talked all night I seem to remember, or as long as the bar was open anyway. To cut a long story very short this lead to Ted becoming a visiting professor at Southampton and to him spending a year with us as a part of a visiting fellowship scheme. It was an amazing year. It was during this year that Ian Heath—one of the original Microcosm team—developed the first version of Cosmic that demonstrated Ted's ideas showing the connections, or links, between the same parallel documents. We could do this in Microcosm because the links were in separable hyperstructure. That bit was easy. The hard bit, as always was, the visualization. Ian did a lot of work on this for Ted to produce the Cosmic book demo.

The other thing that was happening at the time was that the web community had spun away from the hypertext community, and I couldn't get the two communities to work together. The WWW conference had taken on a life of its own and the hypertext community—despite the fact that the Web was really launched at a Hypertext conference—resolutely refused to accept that its future was the Web. We had agreed to host ACM Hypertext'97 in Southampton, and we had lined Ted up as the keynote speaker. I remember saying to Robert Cailliau, who was co-ordinating the Web conference series, "We have fixed our dates, please don't fix the WWW conference for the same week." And sure enough, when the dates for WWW'97 came out there was a complete clash. Bebo White from Stanford was the WWW conference chair. I was so determined to try to make links between the two communities that I negotiated with Bebo for Ted's keynote to be beamed live across the Atlantic and for us to have a joint panel session afterwards. I chaired the panel in Southampton, and Robert chaired the panel in Santa Clara. The technology to achieve this in those days was really very complicated. Dave De Roure managed the technology at our end. I don't know who managed it in the U.S., but it was quite an achievement and it all worked amazingly well.

The Web community is a very different community from the hypertext community culturally, and I don't know how much they understood of what Ted said in his keynote. The most memorable thing for me were the words Ted used to close his keynote—given to a hypertext community in Southampton but addressed to the Web community in Santa Clara—"Your future is my past."

That is so very true, but even now most people in the Web community have no idea just how true it is. As I reflect on how the Web has developed over the last 25 years, I see the ideas that Ted had 30, 40, 50 years ago emerging because they have to emerge. But it's taken a long while, and whilst I love the Web for all it's given us I also understand exactly how it slowed things down as well. I felt this with the Microcosm project too.

There was another major seminal moment for me at WWW'98, which was in Brisbane. Three things happened at that conference as I recall. Tim started talking about the Semantic Web again in his keynote for the conference. He had talked about it at the first WWW conference in 1994 [1] and the idea of making links on data in the information management proposal he wrote in 1989. As far as he was concerned in 1998, the web of linked documents was beginning to emerge but his vision wasn't complete until it was also a web of linked data, and so he started to re-educate the community about this at the Brisbane conference.

Ted was also at the Brisbane conference to pick up a special award. I remember him demoing ZigZag to us in the bar one night at that conference. He was so excited, and we were all mesmerized. So I had heard Tim talk about the Semantic Web and I saw Ted demo ZigZag at the same conference, and I didn't fully appreciate either of them at the time. I understood the principles, but I didn't understand the detail. It's taken me a long time to appreciate both the Semantic Web and ZigZag, but as my understanding of both of them has increased I now firmly believe what I suspected all along: there is a one-to-one correspondence between the two ideas, and that you can implement ZigZag in the RDF graph.

Someday I'll find the time to prove that. I need to get Ted involved in making that happen. I really believe that these two amazing people—Tim and Ted—have the same idea of how you can make links on data to create an incredibly rich hyperstructure for generating knowledge. Tim will never talk about it like that. His idea with the Semantic Web is that machines can, if you describe the data using a vocabulary like an ontology, make inferences about the information contained in the data that couldn't be made in any other way. This is what Ted said in the paper he sent us about his closing keynote for this event, that actually if you take all these ideas to their extreme we will generate more knowledge.

The other thing I remember about the WWW conference in Brisbane is that this is where Sergey Brin and Larry Page published their paper about the algorithm that became the Google search engine. So for me this really was a seminal conference with so many truly ground breaking ideas emerging at the same time, apparently orthogonal to each other but actually all the same thing as time has confirmed, since the Google Knowledge Graph is the Semantic Web or ZigZag by another name. It's all about linking data. This is a much quieter revolution than that initiated by the document Web but it will be much more far reaching. Linked data will become an integral part of the development of data-driven systems architectures that will revolutionize the way we build and maintain information management systems. Linked data architectures will supersede relational databases, make websites easier to build and unify the worlds of hypertext, document management, and databases to create rich interlinked knowledge-based systems as envisaged by the pioneers such as Ted and Doug over 50 years ago.

But the linked data revolution was very slow to take off—largely because it's hard to explain the key concepts to people and what the benefits are. In 2004, it seemed to have completely stalled. Analyzing why this was the case is a much longer story than I have time to tell here, but as a by-product of doing this analysis at the time, Tim, Nigel Shadbolt, Danny Weitzner, and I started to look back at the factors that made the web of linked documents take off in order to try and understand why the web of linked data wasn't. We realized that to understand the ecosystem that is the Web we have to take a socio-technical approach. It cannot just be thought of from the perspective of computer science. For good or bad we called this new approach Web Science, and set about launching a new research and education discipline around this idea. This has been the focus of my work ever since.

I passionately believe that this is a very important new area of study. We work with social scientists and people who understand human and organizational behavior, and it is a very interdisciplinary activity. I spend a lot of time now bringing together different disciplines to study how the Web has emerged, what it means for the future in terms of policy making and what it means for society—how society shapes it as much as how it shapes us. Through the Web Science Trust we organize conferences and workshops, and we have created an international network of web science laboratories. We have also just launched a major new Web Science Institute at Southampton. For me, one of the most exciting things about Web Science is that it attracts as many women as men because it is so interdisciplinary, and so for the first time in my career my classes have as many women as men—unlike the average computer science class! Last year we launched a MOOC (massively open on-line course) in Web Science—a case of using the medium to teach about the medium. If you are interested to learn more, it can be found at http://www.southampton.ac.uk/moocs/webscience.shtml.

Another major project being managed by the Web Science Trust is the development of a distributed global repository of data that people can use to do longitudinal research in this area. The idea is to enable researchers around to the world to share data and data analytics about what is happening on the Web in the same way as the astronomers do with the data they collect from their telescopes. The physicists are trying to explain the mysteries of the physical universe, we are trying to do the same for the digital universe.

What's next? Well, I'm becoming increasingly involved in policy work in areas such as net neutrality, Internet governance, and security, privacy, and trust on the Internet. These are huge issues for us as a global society. I'm a member of the new

Global Commission for Internet Governance being organized by Chatham House and the Canadian Centre for International Governance Innovation. There's talk in the UK of a charter for Internet access rights. The Magna Carta is 800 years old in 2015, so it is very timely to talk about a Magna Carta for the Internet in that year. In these days when we have such tensions between the need for digital surveillance versus the protection of personal privacy on-line, Internet governance is a major topic that needs to be seriously addressed across the world.

As I come to the end of my talk, I want to turn back to the reason why I'm here. I want to pay honor to Ted for so many different reasons. Ted has inspired me throughout my entire career. But it has also been wonderful getting to know him as a person and to be able to talk about Ted and Marlene as two of our closest friends. My husband, Peter, and I have shared some marvelous times with them—one of the most memorable being when we had Doug and Ted and Marlene and Karen to dinner at our house. What an evening! We also have wonderful memories of spending time with them on their houseboat in Sausalito. But there is one memory that just Ted and I share. Ted always works late into the night as I often do. One night we had both been working late at Southampton and long after everyone else had gone home we found ourselves walking out of the office to the car park together. It was midwinter, dark and a bit misty and Ted said to me, "Can you hear the nightingale's singing, Wendy?" Without Ted I would never have noticed them. And that about sums up my career in hypertext. So Ted, thank you for the nightingales and thank you for letting me share your world.

References

1. Berners-Lee T (1994) Plenary at the first World Wide Web Conference. Geneva, Switzerland. http://www.w3.org/Talks/WWW94Tim. Accessed 20 Jan 2015
2. Bush V (1945) As we may think. Atlantic Monthly 176(1):101–108
3. Fountain A, Hall W, Heath I, Davis H (1990). Microcosm: an open model for hypermedia with dynamic linking. Hypertext: concepts, systems and applications: proceedings of the first European conference on hypertext, INRIA, France, November 1990: 298–311. Cambridge University Press
4. Goose S, Dale J, Hill G, de Roure D, Hall W (1996). An open framework for integrating widely distributed hypermedia resources. In: Proceedings of the third IEEE international conference on multimedia computing & systems
5. Nelson TH (1981) Literary machines: the report on, and of, Project Xanadu concerning word processing, electronic publishing, hypertext, thinkertoys, tomorrow's intellectual revolution, and certain other topics including knowledge, education and freedom. Theodor H. Nelson, Swarthmore

Chapter 12
Ted Nelson

Frode Hegland

12.1 Introduction

I'd like to talk about Ted the man, limits, connections, some pretty broad history, all leading up to why I believe Ted is limitless. I was born in Norway. Land of vikings, socially connected politics. Ancestral home of Ted Nelson and Doug Engelbart. A land of fjords. For me the picture has changed to a view of the Thames. I now live in London, greatest city in the world, but I won't go on and on about that.

What I do: I'm a software developer in the school of Doug Engelbart and Ted Nelson. To me, interactivity is paramount – that's what all my work is about. My main project and product is Liquid, which allows you to do useful things directly to selected text in any Mac OS X application. The idea is that when you come across something that sparks your interest, you can act on it immediately, without any real thought or effort. I have started a long term research project and product called Author, which will be a word processor, but not like Word. In a few years, I'll have more to say on that topic.

My other Mac project is LiSA, the Liquid Information Speaking Assistant. She speaks with a real human voice when you get email, saying who the email is from. She not only knows who the message is from, but also whether it's a reply, etc. Not high tech, not a big project, but I mention her here since she's been around since 2001 and sounds wonderful. It's based on super-simple tech: simply pre-recorded voice snippets.

I have also produced a few iOS apps: the major one of which is Interatlas, the first atlas with no visible interface, until you tap an area to see borders. My other iOS apps include the following:

F. Hegland (✉)
10 Elm Lodge, SW6 6NZ London, UK
e-mail: frode@hegland.com

© The Author(s) 2015

D.R. Dechow, D.C. Struppa (eds.), *Intertwingled*, History of Computing,
DOI 10.1007/978-3-319-16925-5_12

1. fleeting moment: which is a hybrid of a still and moving image;
2. flipic: which takes a picture with front and back camera on an iphone at the same time and presents the picture as a 3d 'card';
3. 3dpic: which allows you to take 3D pictures on an iPhone; and
4. Name The Face: an app to help you learn people's names from pictures of their faces.

Finally, I put together The Future of Text Symposium. It has been running for 3 years now. Ted has honoured me by taking part twice. Vint Cerf has also taken part, both as a panelist and sponsor. Academics from The British Museum, The Natural History Museum, Oxford, Princeton, and a number of other institutions have also participated. It's a full day event talking about the future of text: why it's important and how it can develop. The format is as follows:

1. a participant gives a 10 min presentation;
2. the presentation is followed by ten minutes of questions; and
3. then we move on to the next presentation.

It's held each year in the fall, and of course, you are all invited.

12.2   Theodor Holm Nelson

I can't think of Ted without thinking of Marlene, without thinking of them together (Fig. 12.1). So I just want to start by thanking her for also having been such a good friend to me and soulmate to Ted. Thank you Marlene, you are beautiful.

Before I even dare comment on Ted's genius, I just want to thank him for being such a warm and wonderful human being, above all else. Kind, funny, lively! thoughtful, insightful, and committed. You are simply a deep human being.

Fig. 12.1   Ted and Marlene at their farm in New Jersey (2010)

12.3   Limits

I think of Ted as being limitless. Why limitless? Let's look at limits first. Some say that going from a handwritten document to formatted text is progress. Ted would say: Yes. But, he would also add that much as been lost and much, much more can be added. Ted sees the value of what's in between, over and underneath—how things connect. This is how he dreamt up hypertext, which goes so far beyond the typeset page (Fig. 12.2).

WHAT'S LOST: The nuance expressed in the shape of a line, the words deleted in
  edits. Sentences crossed out. Text inserted. Ink blots from late nights working,
  historical coffee stains. The list goes on!
WHAT'S TO BE GAINED: The employment of the power of massively fast,
  massively connected computers.

  I'd like to use the game Battlefield 4 as an example. It's a game that's available on Playstation and PC (available by search on YouTube). This is live game play, this is what the kids (cough, me) play these days. We need to employ this vast computing power and vast networks to augment how we interact with our knowledge—and not just games. And not just Big Data either: all data.

  As for wasted potential, this is Microsoft Word. This is the reality of augmentation today. And this is Word from 1989, which was of course, 25 years ago. Sure, we have bigger screens, but it's the same stuff inside.

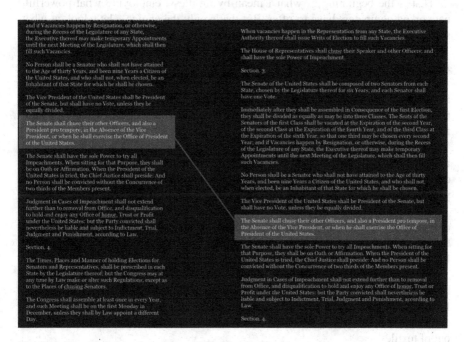

Fig. 12.2 Transcluded section of text of U.S. Constitution

Fig. 12.3 Photograph of a tree, Hyde Park, London, U.K

That is the beginning of what I mean by limitless: employing what powerful, networked computers have to offer. But that's only the engine—let's look at what should be augmented, let's look at what information is. Let's look at connections.

I think Ted's work is limitless because Ted is so obsessed with Connections. And that, is a compliment of the highest order.

Connections. I took a picture (Fig. 12.3) in Green Park in London a few weeks ago. It's a beautiful tree. I used my SONY RX1, VSCO TriX 400 for those of a photographic geek bent. It's quite beautiful don't you think? There is enough framing of the sky and there is a clear trunk to help us see it a tree.

I also took the photo shown in Fig. 12.4. Not quite as clear, not quite as beautiful and more noise than connections right? But when you can interact with it, it conforms to your perspective and it becomes meaningful to you. Interaction gives you ways to understand what's going on, ways to follow connections.

Information comes from connections and the interwinglularity of connections only become meaningful to you when you can follow them. Therefore, I would say the information is interaction, and this is one of the prime insights I have gotten from Ted's work.

Ted is a man rich with intertwingled connections. Ted is very much about the rich tapestry of life. The etymology of tapestry is interesting. From the Proto-Indo-European "to stretch." Poetic. This is what Ted does for us. He stretches and connects. Tapestries are woven, like our stories, like our lives, like the world itself, out of textiles.

Fig. 12.4 Photo of a tree in London's Hyde Park. Excerpted from an animation where the point of view changes

And this leads us gently down the path to the root of the word 'text' itself. It's the same root word as textile—from Latin *textus*, "thing woven," from the past participle of *texere*, "to weave, to join, fit together, braid, interweave, construct, fabricate, build," which is itself from the Proto-Indo-European root *teks*—"to weave, to fabricate, to make."

And then we get to Hypertext: "Text above and beyond the type cast word." All text is woven. All text is connected. Hypertext acknowledges this and frees us from previous artificial constraints.

What I have learnt from Ted is the importance of the understanding that everything is connected and the understanding that to turn this web of actual and potential connections into information, we need to interact with the information richly and powerfully. It's not enough to make 'in-formation' once and then leave it. It needs to be re-in-formable again and again to keep up with human thought and life. Information is interaction.

Information which cannot be interacted with dies. Information which cannot be interacted with is not really information.

I am not going to be going into details on specifics of Ted's work—I don't want to duplicate other presentations here today. I don't think I could add value with this most esteemed academic range of speakers, so I just want to put the importance of Ted's work in a historical perspective instead.

12.4   Historical Perspective

Starting with a question: Is what we have today the ultimate, when it comes to information manipulation? What would you say?

Let's start at the beginning. About 13.7 billion years ago, the universe began. Roughly 4.5 billion years ago, our earth and the planets in our solar system settled into orbits. I wanted to show you this to reflect on the fact that our little planet has been around for about a third of the existence of existence itself. We are of ancient stock. We are a deep part of the deepest history.

After 750 million years or so of our planet merely being pregnant with the possibility of life, self-replicating molecules appear. Life is happening. It's pretty basic, but it's happening. Another 300 million years later, celled life evolves. This is just a billion years after the earths' crust hardened and cooled. Now, for a brief, fleeting moment, *Luca* (last universal common ancestor) lives. And then 7 million years ago, a hominid creature—meaning simply 'human type'—dies in Chad, Africa. We are most definitively human by 200,000 years ago. You would not question the humanity of human being from 200,000 B.C.E. You might feel he or she would be stronger than you or me, but not another species. What if you were confronted with a human being from 100,000 years ago? You would not notice anything different at all.

So, we zoom into the detail of the last few 1,000 years. Çatalhöyük—perhaps the first city—reached its pinnacle 9,000 years ago, with about 7,000 people. We thrived in cities for another 3,000–4,000 years before we invented writing. Printed text has developed over the last 500 years ago, in China and Europe.

I don't to waste your time with the detailed discussions of exactly when interactive text on computer screens happened, many of you here know that better than me, but I like to think of 1968, the year of Doug Engelbart's demo, as a good year. It, of course, has something to do with the fact that that this was the year I was born.

So, before we zoom back out. Let's pause for a second look at today's world. This is our current reality. These are our paradigms: HTML, .doc documents, and WYSIAYG, what Doug called *what you see is ALL you get*. This can't be it people. This can't be the end of what we can develop. By the way, notice how our current paradigms pretty much completely ignores connections.

Right, let's hide the recent past. It's too much of a blink of an eye. Let's move the big picture, down here. So here is big history. Condensed. Abridged. Beginning of the earth here at the left, today at the right. How much future do we have left, (if we don't kill each other)?

For the most basic gauge, the life expectancy of our planet, we have as much time in the future as we have past. The sun, our host planet, is in the middle of its lifespan. Let's zoom out more. This is where our planet fits in the cosmic timeline.

In 100 trillion years, the age of the stars will draw to a close. But even this is not the end of the universe. It's just a phase before it gets more boring. So, my point: we are alive at almost start of the universe if you look at it on this scale. It's the time to look ahead, not to be overly constrained by our teeny history!

It's time to look at the fundamentals. It's time to listen to what the deep thinkers have to say, not be stuck in a paradigm created by simple initial digital commerce. It's time to stop living within the simulations of paper book box of tree corpses in birch coffins. It's time to go past Microsoft Word and similar software packages. The thing with Word is this: Word actively removes connections, actively removes what information is! That. Is. A. Crime.

In dealing with early, less powerful computers and systems, models had to be built to deal with what was once considered large amounts of data. What mattered were "just the facts." This meant only the letters of words were noted down. Not what they looked like, and keeping any kind of a reference as to where they came from became a needless headache. Relationships between documents were lost.

That was then. We no longer have those constraints. It's time to truly value connections. We have to accept our world as being deeply intertwingled. Oh, by the way, did you think I forgot about the Web? I didn't. The web is not a web. The web is not made up of links. A link connects two things. If we hold hands, that's a link.

A URL is more accurately referred to as a "web address," a term which has come about to give *ordinary* people a better impression of what it is going on behind the scene. It's much more accurate to say it's simply an address. To say that it is a pointer-click to something, which may or may not be there, and the thing that is being pointed at does not know what is pointing at it. There is no linking, there is no connection, and there is certainly no transclusion!

So let's praise the web for being a connector 1.0. And now we need to accept that, as much as information itself is interaction, so is life itself. If we fail to focus on interaction of connections, we are building an every larger, but nevertheless, a continually dead environment.

We need to be able to zig-zag through hyperspace at will. I'm sure that you see what I did there. Zig-zagging along aided by Ted's genius of hypertext, Xandau space, and other hyper-Ted thoughts!

12.5   Limitless

THIS is what makes Ted limitless: Ted gives us ways to interact with information by letting us follow connections—the very connections that makes information, information. Ted's work gives us ownership and intimacy with our information. Ted makes our information environments come alive! THIS is what makes Ted limitless. And it can make us limitless too, if we pay attention to the genius of Ted Nelson.

I made a video of my students,[1] the next generation, the people who really matter, and I asked them what they thought about Ted. I hope you will take a look at it.

But before I finish, I have to admit something. My software, particularly Liquid, works well because it integrates neatly into Mac OS X. I have taken the safe route so that my software is quite easy to build. Almost everyone who develops

---

[1] http://youtu.be/e89KwG05xXY

software has. Ted's vision requires much greater re-coding of our basic assumptions and operating environments. So I have to say that if I had the balls and the brains, I wouldn't play it so safe. I would have liked to be more like Ted. Thank you Ted, for being the balls-out brains of our industry!

So that concludes my perspective on Ted, the multifaceted, multitalented, multidimensional man, with so many connections, so much wisdom, inspiration, and insight for all of us.

Chapter 13
History Debugged

Daniel Rosenberg

What does computer work have to say to people outside of computer fields? In what ways do computer fields draw on and contribute to broader intellectual and cultural streams? These are crucial questions today when lives are lived so much in electronic mediation. But they are not new. Questions in information design have played a role in the humanities as long as there have been humanities, from the earliest indexes and diagrams through to Memex, on the cusp of the digitized world we know (Fig. 13.1).

The problem of the relationship between coding and thinking has always been central to the work of Theodor Holm Nelson, and a key aspect of his influence both inside and outside computer fields has been his unwavering insistence on the epistemological consequences of this relationship, often discussed under the rubric he calls "systems humanism." While there is every reason to read Nelson as a figure in the modern history of information theory and design, there are as many reasons to read him in the stream of the contemporary humanities. More concretely, there are excellent reasons to consider Nelson's work—from his earliest efforts such as the literary journal, *Nothing*, through to his visionary samizdat manifesto, *Computer Lib/Dream Machines*, and his recent work reconceptualizing the spreadsheet—as a guide to the universe of paper as it is to that of the screen.

Before I plunge into history before our time, I want to very briefly recall my own first encounter with Ted Nelson's work. It was the late 1990s, an eventful time for computers and for the Internet, days when the phrase "to Google" still merited quotation marks. My own work at that time revolved around the futurisms of eighteenth-century French philosophers and writers, including Denis Diderot (1713–1784), Jean le Rond d'Alembert (1717–1783), Anne-Robert Jacques Turgot (1727–1781), and Louis-Sébastien Mercier (1740–1814), among others.

D. Rosenberg (✉)
Clark Honors College, University of Oregon, 1293, Eugene, OR 97403-1293, USA
e-mail: dbr@uoregon.edu

© The Author(s) 2015
D.R. Dechow, D.C. Struppa (eds.), *Intertwingled*, History of Computing,
DOI 10.1007/978-3-319-16925-5_13

Fig. 13.1 Ted Nelson's Desk. From Nelson, *Computer Lib/Dream Machines* (Courtesy of Theodor Holm Nelson)

That particular year, I had a postdoctoral fellowship at the University of California Humanities Research Institute in Irvine, and my intention was to use the time to write exclusively about the eighteenth century world—and it remained my intention right up until I encountered Ted Nelson's work for the first time, which took me through a garden of forking paths.

That year, I spent a lot of time trying to understand what was happening in the electronic world around me. Imperceptibly at first, my interest in the futurism of the eighteenth century bonded with that of the emergent Web. This also led me to encounter Nelson's work and to a surprising, gratifying, and sustained engagement with it. The research that I published as a result, in a volume entitled *Histories of the Future* [5], was dedicated to Nelson's work (Fig. 13.2).

In the late 1990s, of course, there was much fevered talk about how the world was changing with the advent of new information technologies in general and with the Web in particular. It is not hard to recall the overheated rhetoric of that moment. By the way, I can assure you that one of the many not-new things about our electronic world is its feeling of world-shaking novelty. Here is what Jean-Baptiste Suard (1732–1817), a journalist associate of the French Encyclopedists, had to say about the famous print encyclopedia of Diderot and d'Alembert published between 1751 and 1772:

> What a moment and what an era [the *Encyclopédie*] promised! . . . It was as though its wishes for the human race showed divine force. . . . Nearly drunk with so much hope for the progress of reason, it prophesied a Jerusalem of philosophy that would last more than 1,000 years.[1]

---

[1] P.-J. Garat, *Mémoires historiques sur la vie de M. Suard* (1820), quoted in Daniel Rosenberg, "An Eighteenth-Century Time Machine," in Daniel Gordon, ed., *Postmodernism and the Enlightenment*

Fig. 13.2 In a distant future, an angel rescues Ted Nelson's book from the flood of time. (Adapted from Theodor Holm Nelson Computer Lib/Dream Machines and Balthasar Anton Dunker, Costumes des moeurs et de l'esprit françois avant la grande Révolution à la fin du dix-huitième (1791)). (Credit: Courtesy of Bibliothèque cantonal et universitaire - Lausanne, Switzerland.)

DCXI.

As a reader of eighteenth-century philosophy, literature, and science, the hyperbole of the early age of the Web was nothing if not familiar. Indeed, the echoes of this past were uncanny.

All of which was also somewhat confusing, that is, until I encountered Nelson's books. An iconic image from Nelson's earlier work is shown in Fig. 13.3. Its caption, "everything is deeply intertwingled," is of course, the fulcrum of the current consideration of Nelson's work. And here is something Nelson wrote about it:

> Within bodies of writing, everywhere, there are linkages we tend not to see. The individual document, at hand, is what we deal with; we do not see the total linked collection of them all at once. But they are there, the documents not present as well as those that are, and the grand cat's-cradle among them all. [3]

(New York: Routledge, 2001), 49, and in Bronislaw Backzko, *Utopian Lights: The Evolution of the Idea of Social Progress*, trans. Judith L. Greenberg (New York: Paragon, 1989), 31.

Fig. 13.3 Credit: From
Nelson, *Computer Lib/Dream
Machines* (Courtesy of
Theodor Holm Nelson)

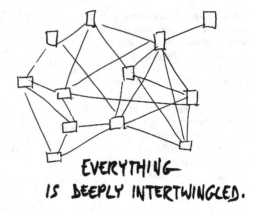

EVERYTHING
IS DEEPLY INTERTWINGLED.

What Ted expressed in this passage from *Literary Machines* resonates strongly with what the Enlightenment philosophers understood the world of paper texts to look like, and, it resonates still more strongly with what they argued it *should* look like.

The philosophers of the Enlightenment understood the problem of knowledge as both a matter of seeing the world in a certain way and also of operationalizing that vision through technical mechanisms. The Enlightenment produced dozens of important new encyclopedias, dictionaries, concordances, atlases, and other interconnecting, non-linear, and non-hierarchical information tools, many of which you are certainly familiar with, even if you don't know much about their origins or early history. All of these eighteenth-century information devices were analog. Nearly all of them, with the exception of a few that had moving parts of one sort or another, ran on the platform of paper. What look to us like elegant, dusty old sets of volumes, looked to the eighteenth-century end user, like genuinely high tech devices. Because they were (Fig. 13.4).

Among the eighteenth-century works to really engage the intertwingling problem, the best, most ambitious, and most thoroughly theorized was certainly the *Encyclopédie: ou Dictionnaire Raisonné des Sciences des Arts et des Métiers* of Denis Diderot and Jean le Rond d'Alembert. The *Encyclopédie* was remarkable in every way. It was brilliant, employing the labors of the best writers of its day including luminaries such as Voltaire (1694–1778) and Jean-Jacques Rousseau (1712–1778). It was enormous, comprising 28 volumes, 72,000 articles by over 2,000 writers, and more than 3,000 plates. And it was formally rigorous, employing new systems of reference and cross-reference, making it as accessible as it was sophisticated. It was also, not incidentally, a great gesture of free-thinking, and for this it was censored, though the French censor in fact liked it very much and turned a blind eye when the work was smuggled into France.

The formal reference system embedded in the work was no mere convenience. Quite the opposite: Diderot and d'Alembert believed that their encyclopedia offered a response to an emerging crisis in the general field of information. Among other challenges, there was the perception of information explosion. The eighteenth-century world was awash in newspapers, journals, letters, bureaucratic documents, and books. Books, books, and more books. So many, it seemed, that contemporaries despaired at the prospect of mastering them all [4].

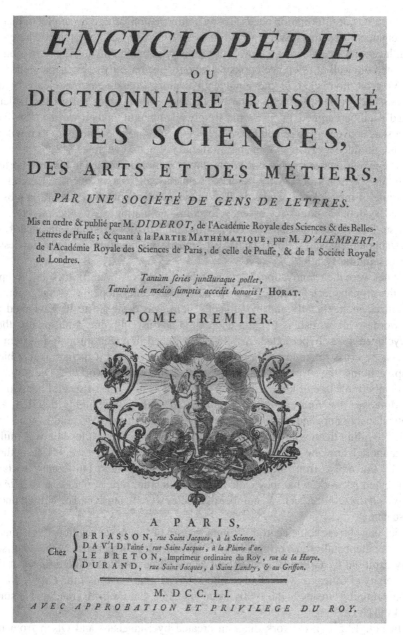

Fig. 13.4 Frontispiece from the *Encyclopédie* of Diderot and d'Alembert (1751–1772) (Credit: Encyclopédie, ou Dictionnaire raisonné des sciences, des arts et des métiers, ed. by Denis Diderot and Jean le Rond d'Alembert)

In order to perceive the visceral dimension of this problem, you have to understand that, through the end of the seventeenth century, scholars continued to maintain the fiction that a true polymath could and should master all important literature, much as we still very recently imagined that brick and mortar libraries could effectively serve our information needs. Today's information vertigo is parallel to that of the eighteenth century. Every period feels that it overloads something. The eighteenth century experienced a blowout of individual human memory, and in a flash, invented the wall of reference books we've only just recently seen dismantled.

As print flourished in the eighteenth century, the mnemonic ideals of the Renaissance seemed farther and farther distant. Without some sort of fix, Diderot and d'Alembert argued, books would simply pile up until, in their words, "It will be almost as convenient to search for some bit of truth concealed in nature as it will be to find it hidden away in an immense multitude of bound volumes." [2].

Their solution was qualitatively different from those proposed in our own period, including Nelson's design for Xanadu. Xanadu calls for an open and emergent structure of interlinked documents. The Encyclopedists, by contrast, built a mostly closed system: a single set of encyclopedias, emulating a literary universe. Of course, Diderot and d'Alembert built in mechanisms for external reference, revision, supplement, and so forth, but they designed the *Encyclopédie* to run flawlessly as freestanding system.

What were their innovations? Among others, they borrowed for their encyclopedia the alphabetical format of a dictionary. Older encyclopedias were generally organized hierarchically and by subject. Theirs was designed to be navigated by keyword, to allow readers to enter and exit at any useful point. Additionally, their encyclopedia was hypertexted. Articles were linked in a web through a system of *renvois* or cross-references. The *Encyclopédie* also offered a hierarchical subject map, echoing the structure of older works, but, in the work of Diderot and d'Alembert, the tree of knowledge was presented as only one of several heuristics.

Moreover, the *Encyclopedie* was illustrated with lavish, highly detailed, and meticulously annotated diagrams illustrating articles in the work and at the same time providing them with a visual index. Finally, the new encyclopedia was multiply authored, drawing on famous and obscure writers across many fields. Its authority did not derive from the prestige of a single great mind but from a socially distributed network, what they called, in an influential turn of phrase, a *société de gens de lettres*. Indeed, a large number of articles were unattributed or written under false names.

For our purposes, the central defining feature of this new encyclopedia is that it was, fundamentally and originally, conceptualized as hypertext, a characteristic ably explored by Gilles Blanchard and Mark Olsen at the ARTFL project at the University of Chicago, which had an interactive, digital version of the *Encyclopédie* up and running already in the 1990s around the time that I was first reading Nelson's books [1].

In Fig. 13.5 is a network diagram created by Blanchard and Olsen from the ARTFL *Encyclopédie* displaying the direction and density of some of the cross-references embedded in the work. This network diagram itself is, of course, not an artifact from the eighteenth century. At the same time, this modern diagram expresses a thoroughly conceptualized design logic implicit in the system of cross-references of the *Encyclopédie*. In the diagram, nodes represent topics identified by Diderot and d'Alembert; fatter lines show a higher number of links. The visual logic

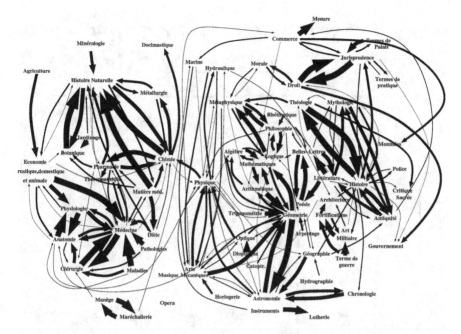

Fig. 13.5 Map of renvois (cross-references) in the *Encyclopédie* of Diderot and d'Alembert by Mark Olsen and Gilles Blanchard (Credit: Courtesy of Mark Olsen and Gilles Blanchard)

of the diagram makes a strong contrast with the familiar branching tree diagram favored by the Encyclopedists as a mechanism for expressing a hierarchical relationship among academic disciplines. This very real contrast, however, should not be understood as a contradiction. The Encyclopedists understood hierarchy and intertwingulation as complementary and mutually inflecting perspectives. Each buttressed and improved the other (Fig. 13.6).

There is a great deal to say about the specific features of eighteenth-century thought illuminated by these diagrams. But above all, we see clearly that the hierarchical distribution of knowledge which many have considered paradigmatic of Enlightenment epistemology, is not only a pale shadow of the complexity present in it but is also a poor representation of what scholars and philosophers of the Enlightenment understood themselves to be doing. The Encyclopedists employed a system of cross-reference in order to solve a problem related to the actual complexity of knowledge while at the same time enabling new kinds of understanding and inquiry that were hampered by older literary conventions.

The Encyclopedists understood their project as both urgent and revolutionary. In their view, modern science and philosophy required a new interdisciplinary approach. Boundaries among the various arts and sciences were collapsing, and continued progress would only be possible with a further demolition of disciplines. Though Olsen and Blanchard's network diagram would not have been familiar to the generation of the Encyclopedists, the concepts behind it were. They too were

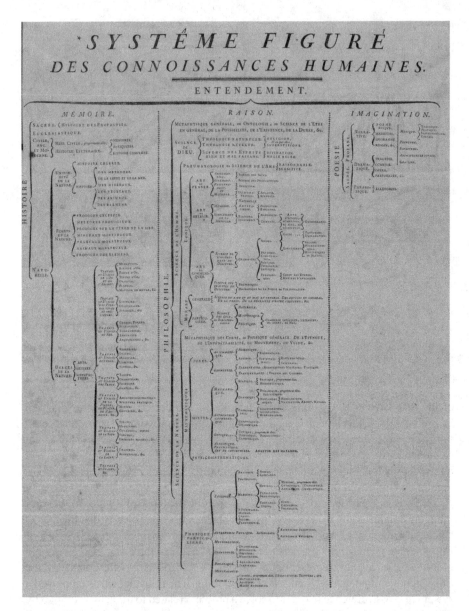

Fig. 13.6 Système figuré des connaissances humaines from the *Encyclopédie* of Diderot and d'Alembert (1751–72) (Credit: Encyclopédie, ou Dictionnaire raisonné des sciences, des arts et des métiers, ed. by Denis Diderot and Jean le Rond d'Alembert)

thinking about intellectual phenomena in terms of underlying structures and aggregate relationships.

In the *Chart of Biography* from 1765 (Fig. 13.7), for example, the renowned English scientist and theologian Joseph Priestley depicted the history of the arts and sciences as an "immense river" of time carrying along many individual contributors.

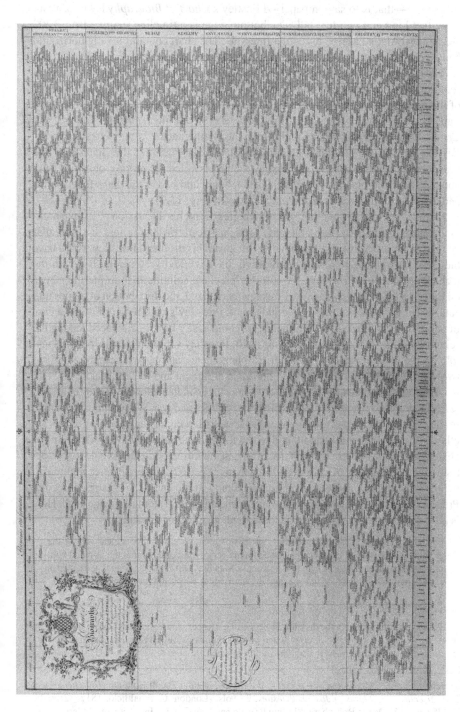

Fig. 13.7 Joseph Priestley, *Chart of Biography* (1765) (Credit: Courtesy of the Library Company of Philadelphia)

In real life—that is to say on paper—Priestley's *Chart of Biography* is large, about three feet long and two feet tall. The bottom edge is a timeline running from 1200 BC to 1800 AD, measured in regular intervals. The chart contains six big horizontal bands, each devoted to a general *category* of achievement [6].

The categories themselves are a fascinating artifact of their time, and a good reminder that, as many affinities as we may find between our world and the world of the eighteenth century, these are different times. In the top band of the chart, we find the Historians, Antiquaries, and Lawyers; below them are the Orators and Critics; then come the Artists and Poets; the Mathematicians and Physicians; the Divines and Metaphysicians; and finally at the very bottom, the Statesmen and Warriors. The interior area of Priestley's chart is filled to varying densities with about 2,000 solid black horizontal lines that begin and end at the dates for the birth and death of the figures depicted in the diagram (Fig. 13.7).

Priestley's system is another sort of hypertext. And his discussion of its hypertextual features is explicit. Each of the life lines on Priestley's chart refers to a particular person, as indicated by a name above it. But, given his druthers, Priestley would have hidden the names. A rollover feature might have worked very nicely. But with the technology of print, Priestley saw no other practical solution than to put the names on the chart in a very tiny font. As Priestley recognized, the distribution of names into categories was based on subjective judgment. Priestley's own biography was a case in point. A great figure in several fields, he could easily have been placed among the scientists or the theologians of his time. Still, Priestley ventured that the patterns visible on the chart revealed real historical phenomena, among which he highlighted two. And these will bring us back to our main argument and to Ted Nelson.

First, Priestley notes a difference between patterns in fields for the history of art and science compared with those for the history of politics and war. We see this for example in the contrast between the range devoted to the Mathematicians and Physicians (in other words, the scientists) and that devoted to the Statesmen and Warriors. From the changing densities of achievement discovered in the former, Priestley is able to spin out a story of the Classical, Medieval, and Renaissance periods. From the latter, nothing. In the realm of politics and war, from the beginning to the end of the historical record, Priestley finds abundance everywhere and no meaningful, patterned change at all. Here is how Priestley puts it, in a passage that I think it still resonates today:

> By the several void spaces between . . . groups of great men, we have a clear idea of the great revolutions of all kinds of *science*, from the very origin of it; so that the thin and void places in the chart are, in fact, no less instructive than the most crowded, in giving us an idea of the great interruptions of science, and the intervals at which it hath flourished.

By contrast, he says,

> We see no void spaces in the division of Statesmen, Heroes, and Politicians. The world hath never wanted competitors for empire and power, and least of all in those periods in which the sciences and the arts have been the most neglected.[2]

---

[2] Joseph Priestley, *Description of a Chart of Biography*, in John Towill Rutt, ed., *The Theological and Miscellaneous Works of Joseph Priestley*, 25 vols. (London: G. Smallfield, 1817–32) v. 24, p. 475 quoted in Daniel Rosenberg, "Joseph Priestley and the Graphic Invention of Modern Time," *Studies in Eighteenth Century Culture* 36 (2007): 68.

This was 1765. Not bad at all, I'd say.

Priestley's second point, closely related, is that historical advance in the arenas of art and science is not only real, it is also, finally, inevitable. For some in Priestley's period, this idea, the idea of progress, was a matter of faith. Priestley thought it was nothing more than a statistically supported analysis of history, an analysis embedded in the chart itself.

Priestley believed that the largest present impediment to progress in ideas was the cloistering of knowledge within small domains, whether languages, nations, or disciplines. He argued that his chart showed that by the latter part of the eighteenth century, all of those barriers were falling and the acceleration of progress had become irresistible. And yet, there were dilemmas. As we know so well in our own period, acceleration of information production brings problems all its own. And this is one of the reasons why we find in the eighteenth century such a tremendous diversity of works employing new strategies of data compression and display such as the *Chart of Biography* and the *Encyclopédie*, themselves.

I don't want to overstate the resemblance between the eighteenth-century moment and our own. There is a resemblance. However what matters is not similarity but connection. The textual strategies of the eighteenth-century encyclopedia and the display strategies of eighteenth-century infographics are only two examples of a very large set of information tools that we not only continue to use today—and by the way, many other staples of our infographics such as the line graph and the bar chart are eighteenth-century confections—but that we think of, in their re-invented electronic form, as hallmarks of our own information consciousness.[3]

Part of what has always set Ted Nelson's work apart is its sensitivity such to historical predecessors. Nelson's has always been a distinctive futurism, rich in appreciation of what works in traditional information mechanisms (and especially those of the paper world), yet impatient with dogmatism and with low-dimensional approaches to knowledge. For me, the key to Nelson's work has always been his aphorism "Literature is debugged" [3].

The idea, deceptive in its simplicity, is that literature in its most "traditional" sense embodies and operationalizes any number of systems that may be theoretical, social, linguistic, and above all textual, that, whatever else we may say about them, they have proven, over the course of centuries, functional, durable, and adaptable. In other words, they have *worked*. This is a good quality for any technology.

To paraphrase Louis-Sébastien Mercier—one of our eighteenth-century informants and, not incidentally, author of one of the world's first future fictions, *L'an 2440, rêve s'il en fut jamais* (1769)—it is a dream if there ever was one, the notion that an information system we build today could still be running three hundred or

---

[3] Early modern antecedents to today's information universe are explored in different respects in many recent works including Ann Blair, *Too Much to Know: Managing Scholarly Information Before the Information Age* (New Haven: Yale University Press, 2010); Markus Krajewski, *Paper Machines: About Cards & Catalogs, 1548–1929*, trans. Peter Krapp (Cambridge: MIT Press, 2011); Edward Tufte, *The Visual Display of Quantitative Information* (Cheshire, CT: Graphics Press, 1993).

more years from now. And yet this is the case for printed reference works, of which eighteenth-century encyclopedias and timelines are great monuments.

The notion that "literature is debugged," then, should not be taken to mean that "traditional" literature or literary systems are problem-free. In fact, Nelson's books all contain strenuous critiques of received practices, foremost among them, that of presenting information in inflexible hierarchical and linear structures. Nelson has sometimes grouped these criticisms under a rubric he calls the "school problem." [3] The Encyclopedists, thinking in parallel terms, called it the problem of "scholasticism." For them, as for Nelson, Aristotle was one of the principal demons to slay.

The scholastic attitude is sometimes embodied in *textual forms*, but, as the non-linear and interlinking structure of the eighteenth-century encyclopedia demonstrates, it is in no way inherent to print. As I have already suggested, there are dozens, even hundreds, of examples, of traditional textual and diagrammatic forms designed specifically to facilitate non-linear and non-hierarchical thinking. Yet regular discourse, as was implicit in my previous sentence, shows off these very same characteristics. As Nelson [3] points out,

> Many people consider [hypertext] to be new and drastic and threatening. However, I would like to take the position that hypertext is fundamentally traditional and in the mainstream of literature. Customary writing chooses one expository sequence from among the possible myriad; hypertext allows many, all available to the reader. In fact, however, we constantly depart from sequence, citing things ahead and behind in the text. Phrases like "as we have already said" and "as we will see" are really implicit pointers to contents elsewhere in the sequence.

Among technical devices designed to facilitate the sort of jumping that narrative language performs as a matter of course (though with limited flexibility) one might mention, for example, indexes, tables, file cards, and so forth. And of course, contemporary information designers *do* think about all of these things. Nelson's own recent efforts to reimagine database design fall into this category of work. All of this was prefigured in his print works from the multiply-folded *Nothing* literary magazine he published at Swarthmore to the hopscotched, inverted, and mutually dependent texts of *Computer Lib/Dream Machines*, to the choose-your-own-adventure numbering of *Literary Machines*, as well as the tea leaf patterns of Xanadu and the fractal explosions of ZigZag.

The phrase, "literature is debugged," should not be taken to mean that we cannot improve on old systems, but rather, that it is essential to notice *how*, for better and worse, old systems function. This is, of course, the sort of thing a historian is not unhappy to contemplate (Fig. 13.8).

There is so much that we can and must take from Nelson's writing. For me, Nelson's work functions as an injunction to attend to our information ancestors, while not indulging in worship. For humanists, in general, I think it should be read as a call to study old literatures *as systems*, something an encouraging number of humanities scholars are now beginning to do.

Fig. 13.8 The Apotheosis of Computer Lib (Credit: Adapted from Theodor Holm Nelson, Computer Lib/Dream Machines and Encyclopédie, ou Dictionnaire raisonné des sciences, des arts et des métiers, ed. by Denis Diderot and Jean le Rond d'Alembert)

References

1. Blanchard G, Olsen M (2002) Le système de renvoi dans l'Encyclopédie: Une cartographie des structures de connaissances au XVIIIe siècle. Recherches sur Diderot et sur l'Encyclopédie 31–32:45–70
2. Diderot D (1751–72) Encyclopédie. In: Diderot D, d'Alembert JLR (eds) Encyclopédie, ou Dictionnaire Raisonné des Sciences, des Arts et des Métiers par une Société de Gens de Lettres
3. Nelson TH (1981) Literary machines: The report on, and of, Project Xanadu concerning word processing, electronic publishing, hypertext, Thinkertoys, tomorrow's intellectual revolution, and certain other topics including knowledge, education and freedom. Theodor H. Nelson, Swarthmore
4. Rosenberg D (2003) Early modern information overload. J Hist Ideas 64:1–9
5. Rosenberg D (2005) Electronic memory. In: Daniel Rosenberg and Susan Harding (eds) Histories of the future. Duke University Press, Durham, pp 125–52
6. Rosenberg D, Grafton A (2010) Cartographies of time. Princeton Architectural Press, New York

Chapter 14
We Can and Must Understand Computers NOW

Noah Wardrip-Fruin

14.1 Three Phrases

From the endlessly quotable Ted Nelson—whose neologisms pepper the language we use to understand the present, from "hypertext" to "visualization"—perhaps no phrase is better known than, "You Can and Must Understand Computers NOW." It was emblazoned across the *Computer Lib* side of his 1974 *Computer Lib/Dream Machines* (*CL/DM*), the most influential book in the history of computational media.[1]

Nelson's call is not only memorable today, but still quite relevant. For example, consider the recent revelations of massive government surveillance, as disclosed by Edward Snowden and others. Without a deep understanding of computing, one might debate whether the vision of Total Information Awareness is morally right, or is instead sending us down a path to an "Orwellian," *1984*-style future. However, with a deep understanding of computing, one can not only raise the questions of morality in more depth, but one can also see that Total Information Awareness is a technically unworkable fantasy (like the Star Wars program pursued by the Reagan administration in the non-fictional 1980s) providing a false rationale for treating everyone as a suspect.

In other words, one reason that we must understand computers now is so that we can understand what is happening, and make informed choices, as members of a computationally-steeped democracy. We need to understand computing so that we can see past deceptions about what computers can do, and how computers work. As

---

[1] For example, as Steve Wozniak said at Intertwingled, "At our computer club, the bible was *Computer Lib*" — referring to the Homebrew Computer Club, from which Apple Computer and other major elements of the turn to personal computers emerged [18].

N. Wardrip-Fruin (✉)
Department of Computational Media, University of California, Santa Cruz,
1156 High Street, MS:SOE3, Santa Cruz, CA 95064, USA
e-mail: nwf@soe.ucsc.edu

© The Author(s) 2015
D.R. Dechow, D.C. Struppa (eds.), *Intertwingled*, History of Computing,
DOI 10.1007/978-3-319-16925-5_14

Nelson puts it colorfully, "Down with cybercrud!" However, that is not the only reason we must understand computers.

In thinking about the other reasons we must understand computers, and in considering a variety of projects and ideas that have sought to help an understanding of computing become more widespread, I believe we should also attend to two further phrases from *CL/DM*—neither as well known, but each extremely telling. The first, also from the 1974 edition, is, "presentation by computer is a branch of show biz and writing, not of psychology, engineering or pedagogy" [10, DM2]. The second, added in the 1987 edition, is, "All Simulation is Political" [11, CL149].

I choose these two additional phrases, in part, because they point to ideas of Nelson's that have deeply shaped my own thinking and career—a career in computational media that came into focus after I found a copy of *CL/DM* in my college bookstore. A piece like this one could be written about other facets of my thinking, using a different selection of *CL/DM* phrases, and I believe the same is true for many of the most insightful people I've met in the field—that their thinking was indelibly shaped by an early encounter with Nelson's ideas. But for telling this story, let me begin with "You Can and Must Understand Computers NOW."

14.2 We Can and Must

Nelson is certainly not alone in calling for broad understanding of computing, in some form, and not the first to do so. The earliest example I can find is Alan Perlis's call—in 1961—for all university Frosh to take a programming class [12]. This is pretty obscure. A much better known example is the Logo project (often remembered for its "turtle" graphics) created by Seymour Papert, Wallace Feurzeig, Daniel Bobrow, and collaborators beginning in 1966 [2]. A more recent example is Jeannette Wing's call for broad "computational thinking," which she characterizes as a set of conceptual tools for "solving problems, designing systems, and understanding human behavior" [17].

These sorts of undertakings are generally noble projects. But I would argue that, at root, many aren't actually about people understanding computers (it is closer to a side effect) and they certainly aren't about what Nelson is calling for. In "Logo: A Project History" Anit Chakraborty, Randy Graebner, and Tom Stocky write, "the original Logo developers were out to change mathematics by helping children improve problem solving abilities" (1999). Similarly, as a 2012 report from the UK's Royal Society notes, computational thinking is primarily about thinking like a computer scientist in a wide variety of contexts, rather than understanding computers in Nelson's sense.[2]

---

[2] "Computational thinking is the process of recognising aspects of computation in the world that surrounds us, and applying tools and techniques from Computer Science to understand and reason about both natural and artificial systems and processes" [5].

14.3 Show Biz and Writing

In the introductory pages of *Dream Machines,* Nelson makes it clear why *CL/DM* is a book with two sides. He does not aim for broader understanding of computers, through the information found in *Computer Lib,* simply because our society is becoming more computational in general. Rather, as he writes:

> My special concern, all too tightly framed here, is the use of computers to help people write, think, and show. But I think presentation by computer is a branch of show biz and writing, not of psychology, engineering or pedagogy. This would be idle disputation if it did not have far-reaching consequences for the designs of the systems we are all going to have to live with. [10, DM2]

In other words, we all must understand computers not just because computers are important, but because the media of the future (and now the present) are computational. We need people who are able to understand, work in, and invent computational media—media that, in Nelson's words, continue the traditions of "literature, film and scholarship"—and are able to do so with, "art, zest, intelligence, and the highest possible ideals" [10, DM2]. This is very much not the same thing as thinking mathematically, or thinking like a computer scientist.

Luckily, there is a tradition of work that takes media and literacy more seriously. The Smalltalk programming language was developed in the 1970s by Alan Kay, Dan Ingalls, Adele Goldberg, and others [6]. Together with the vision of the Dynabook personal computer, it presented an approach to computing that focused on reading and writing (that is to say, computational literacy) and the creation of media and media-making tools (including simulations). And a number of the descendants of Smalltalk and Logo are concerned with media-making and broadening literacy, such as the Processing language for artists and designers, the Scratch language that uses snap-together tiles, and the games-focused Kodu language [7, 13, 14]. There is also conceptual work that seems to foreground literacy issues, as seen in the "computational literacy" discussed in Andrea diSessa's book *Changing Minds* [3].

But here, as with much else in *CL/DM,* Nelson's warning proves prescient. While what we need is a convergence of computing with the arts and humanities, what we get is more often "psychology, engineering or pedagogy." diSessa's book, for example, is primarily concerned with science education, rather than literacy as understood in the traditions of literature, film, and scholarship. More broadly, much of the Human-Computer Interaction community seems convinced that compelling computational media forms can be discovered and designed through psychology-style experiments. Attempts to move computational media forward through pure engineering approaches, in areas such as computer graphics, give us awful "photorealistic" films such as 2007's *Beowulf*—while those few who understand that computing and art must work together (that high-level technical goals cannot be set or evaluated apart from artistic goals) create much stronger, more stylized animations such as 2008's *WALL-E.*[3]

---

[3] "Computational Media" has recently emerged as a name for the type of work that performs this interdisciplinary integration [15].

Happily, some of the work that follows Logo and Smalltalk does come from those who understand these issues, and are themselves media makers. Ben Fry and Casey Reas, the initiators of Processing, are an accomplished artist and information designer. Matt MacLaurin and Stephen Coy, key creators of Kodu, are both game industry veterans. Projects like these succeed at creating media-centric environments that broaden the ability to understand computers and make computational media—and they do so by embedding media-making knowledge from their creators into computational structures.

But that is not all that is embedded.

14.4 All Simulation Is Political

In the 1987 edition of *CL/DM,* Nelson adds a section with the headline, "All Simulation Is Political." He writes below it:

> Every simulation program, and thus every simulation, has a *point of view.* Just like a statement in words about the world, it is a *model* of how things are, with its own implicit emphases: it highlights some things, omits others, and always simplifies. The future projections made by a simulation only project those views forward in time. [11, CL149]

In the kinds of media made with Kodu and Scratch (and many other related systems, such as Alice, Squeak, and AgentSheets) *simulation* is a primary form of representation. The world is represented through rules and the interaction of (and our interactions with) those rules over time, together with data that represents the world state and constants.

As Nelson observes, all the simulations created with these systems embed assumptions about the world that derive from viewpoints—they are political. Similarly, systems for creating simulations are also based on assumptions, derived from viewpoints.

In an individual simulation we see the politics in the rules and data. In a system for creating simulations we see the politics in the available elements and process of creation. In both cases, the politics are often implicit and unconscious.

Consider the Kodu system.[4] Kodu focuses on making games, and has a model of agent-oriented programming (using robotics-style sensors and actions) that can be carried out with an Xbox controller. Almost everything is menu driven, and many problems that plague beginning programmers (such as syntax errors) are effectively eliminated by the system's approach. By programming different agents to interact with each other and the environment, an autonomous simulation can be created. But Kodu's tutorials focus instead on game projects, leaving one or more agent(s) under the control of a player. Everything created is rendered in smooth 3D, often using professional models and textures included with Kodu—creating a sense of polish

---

[4] Kodu is both an influential system itself and the basis of Microsoft's Project Spark, launched in October 2014.

for even the simplest project, and making even the sculpting of the environments in which agents interact an appealing activity for many in the target age group (roughly 7–14, though with an emphasis on the upper end of the range).

In a menu-based system such as Kodu, perhaps the simplest way to surface some of its assumptions, and therefore its politics, is to look at the menu structure. Kodu's menus are hierarchical, with the elements on the top level the fastest to discover and use, presumably reflecting assumptions about what will be most useful. Here are some observations about Kodu's menus:

- Shooting is one of a handful of actions in the top-level menu.
- Being shot is one of a handful of sensors in the top-level menu.
- Saying something is in a sub-menu.
- No menu items support an internal life for characters, or social relationships between characters.

We might ask ourselves, does this really reflect the range of what a diverse group of early teenagers would care about, and want to represent about the world? Of course not. It reflects particular interests—and the male-dominated subgroup most interested in them is not one underrepresented in computing. In other words, despite the nobility of the project, the implicit politics of Kodu's menus of actions and sensors is the politics of the status quo—shaping what can be said, and who can say it, along familiar lines. In this it is far from alone.

14.5 Understand Computers How?

While in theory we could create computational media about anything that we could write about, or make a film about, in practice our tools and established genres generally support a much narrower range. In a sense we live in the world Nelson warned about, in which the designs of the systems we live with do not support broad thinking, expression, and innovation.

But I write about Kodu in this chapter because, when I was part of a group that approached the Kodu team, we found a genuine interest in shifting its expressive range. We worked primarily with Matt MacLaurin, Brad Gibson, and Kent Foster at Microsoft (Kodu emerged from Microsoft's FUSE Labs and Microsoft Research). Our team included Teale Fristoe, Jill Denner, Michael Mateas, Brandon Tearse, Larry LeBron, Eric Kaltman, and Gina Lepore (all from UC Santa Cruz or ETR Associates).[5]

We did some simple things, like adding an easy way for characters to listen for language (not just speak it) which became part of the main Kodu distribution. But

---

[5] The first stage of our work is described in "Say it With Systems" [4]. The project was supported in part by the National Science Foundation (under Grant No. DRL-1042944). However, any opinions, findings, and conclusions or recommendations expressed in this material are those of the author and do not necessarily reflect the views of the National Science Foundation.

we also experimented with more complex changes, such as giving characters different levels of friendship, and creating sensors and actions that made it possible for agents to alter and respond to these levels. We worked to make these almost as simple to use as those for shooting and being shot, and we rearranged the menus so that they were at the same level. We created new curricula, introducing Kodu in new ways, and new sample games, emphasizing our new sensors and actions. We did all this in the context of talking with early teens from a variety of socio-economic backgrounds, and we ran after-school programs in a variety of middle schools, using versions of Kodu iterated between each program.

What we found, perhaps unsurprisingly, is that by the end we were seeing a much wider variety of games. There were more types of play, and a broader range of subject matters. In fact, what we eventually found was that Kodu's visual polish—an important part of its initial appeal—became one of the barriers. Its models and animations were created for a system that made shooting and racing gameplay easy. When teens started considering making a broader set of games, they saw a mismatch between their potential game systems and the ways the games could appear on screen. But in a sense, when teens observed this it was also positive. It was the beginning of a critique of the assumptions built into Kodu's available elements, opened by shifting the available rules without shifting the data.

To my knowledge, what we did with Kodu has not been done with any other tool. Current tools and ideas may aim to broaden understanding of computing, they may focus on computational media literacy, and they may embody lessons learned from media making. But they are divorced from critical thinking about their representations—from point of view, from politics. They haven't been critiqued regarding the way their technical specifics connect to ideas of the world, much less reshaped in response to critique.

When this is how we do work in our field, we run a significant risk. We run the risk that all these well-intentioned projects end up solving precisely the wrong problem. Nelson did not say that we can and must understand computers because the IT sector (or the surveillance state, or Walmart) has an urgent need for more computing-literate worker bees. Nelson's challenge is only answered if we educate people who are prepared to disrupt business as usual—and to invent the broad, thoughtful media of the future.

14.6 Reading and Writing

Putting Nelson's three statements together, we see an urgent call for a creative and critical literacy of computing broadly, and computational media in particular. This call is as pressing today as it was when *CL/DM* was first published.

Thinking in terms of critical literacy also reveals something rather odd about most attempts to broaden understanding of computing. They are almost entirely focused on *writing,* on the construction of computational artifacts (whether through textual code, Kodu menus, Scratch blocks, or some other means). But this is not the approach we use with other forms of critical literacy. We don't assume, for example, that someone who is going to "read and write" the language of cinema should be concerned solely with shooting and editing their own films, never watching and critically interpreting existing films.

Of course, there are those who have addressed, or at least identified, this gap. Michael Mateas's call for "procedural literacy" is an early call for a critical literacy for computational media makers [8]. Ian Bogost's "procedural rhetoric" draws on the history of rhetoric for a model of critically understanding and making processes [1].

And in recent years work on critical interpretation of computing, taking the technical level seriously, has blossomed. The MIT Press has been one of the leading supporters of this, initiating new book series in both software studies and platform studies. However, this critical *reading* generally still remains divorced from *writing*. I know of no educational institution that teaches them together (e.g., no introductory programming course that includes introductory software studies content) and I know of only one published scholarly book that includes the writing of software as one of the critical methods it uses in analyzing software (the unusually-titled *10 PRINT CHR$(205.5 + RND(1)); : GOTO 10* [9]).

Of course, while undertakings such as software studies seem new to many, for those of us who read Nelson's work it is simply the continuation of his tradition. *CL/DM* contains much that is clearly the critical interpretation of software, connecting the technical level to the cultural one—ranging from discussing the "drill and practice" assumptions built into the TUTOR programming language to exposing the simple workings of *Eliza* and other systems used to market artificial intelligence ideas [10, DM27, DM14]. It is heartening to see the continuation of this work finally being taken up by a wider group, and we can only hope that it is increasingly brought together with attempts to broaden the writing side of a creative and critical computational literacy.

14.7 Conclusion

I'm deeply honored to have the opportunity to contribute to this volume, just as I was honored to have the opportunity to help bring Nelson's writing to a new generation when he gave permission for sections of *CL/DM* and other texts to be reprinted in *The New Media Reader* [16]. While Nelson's work is certainly of historical importance, it also has much to tell us in the present—providing a necessary perspective for evaluating what we are doing in the field, and pointing in directions of great importance for us to pursue. I hope that this chapter provides a useful example of one way this has been done.

I also hope that the broader implications of the lessons I draw from selecting the three highlighted *CL/DM* phrases are clear. To put them another way: If we educate everyone to think creatively and critically about and with computational media, we will also be educating them to think critically about computing—to read simulations for their biased assumptions, to know that warrantless wiretapping of every citizen is not only wrong, but pointless, and more. And that, I believe, is the way in which *we can and must understand computers now.*

References

1. Bogost I (2007) Persuasive games: the expressive power of videogames. MIT Press, Cambridge, MA
2. Chakraborty A, Graebner R, Stocky T (1999) "LOGO: a project history." Website for the structure of engineering revolutions, Mindell DA (ed). December 1999. http://web.mit.edu/6.933/www/LogoFinalPaper.pdf
3. DiSessa AA (2001) Changing minds: computers, learning, and literacy. MIT Press, Cambridge, MA
4. Fristoe T, Denner J, MacLaurin M, Mateas M (2011) Say it with systems: expanding Kodu's expressive power through gender-inclusive mechanics. In: Proceedings of the 6th international conference on foundations of digital games, ACM, pp 227–234
5. Furber S (2012) Shut down or restart? The way forward for computing in UK schools. The Royal Society, London
6. Kay AC (1996) The early history of Smalltalk. In: History of programming languages—II. ACM, pp 511–598
7. MacLaurin, MB (2011) The design of Kodu: a tiny visual programming language for children on the Xbox 360. ACM Sigplan Notices 46(1):241–246. ACM
8. Mateas M (2005) Procedural literacy: educating the new media practitioner. On Horiz 13(2):101–111
9. Montfort N, Baudoin P, Bell J, Bogost I, Douglass J, Marino MC, Mateas M, Reas C Sample M, Vawter N (2012) 10 PRINT CHR $(205.5+ RND (1));: GOTO 10. The MIT Press, Cambridge, MA
10. Nelson TH (1974) Computer lib: dream machines. Self published
11. Nelson TH (1987) Computer lib: dream machines. Tempus Books of Microsoft Press, Redmond
12. Perlis AJ (1961) The role of the digital computer in the university. Comput Autom 10(4 &4B):10–15
13. Reas C, Fry B (2006) Processing: programming for the media arts. AI Soc 20(4):526–538
14. Resnick M, Maloney J, Monroy-Hernández A, Rusk N, Eastmond E, Brennan K, Millner A et al (2009) Scratch: programming for all. Commun ACM 52(11):60–67
15. Wardrip-Fruin N, Mateas M (2014) Envisioning the future of computational media: the final report of the media systems project. Center for Games and Playable Media, UC, Santa Cruz
16. Wardrip-Fruin N, Montfort N (eds) (2003) The new media reader. MIT Press, Cambridge, MA
17. Wing JM (2006) Computational thinking. Commun ACM 49(3)
18. Wozniak S (2014) In "Intertwingled: afternoon session #2." Chapman University, Orange, California. Video timecode: 58:14. http://ibc.chapman.edu/Mediasite/Play/52694e57c4b546f0ba8814ec5d9223ae1d

Chapter 15
The Future of Transclusion

Robert M. Akscyn

15.1   Introduction

Transclusion, a term coined by Ted Nelson [5, 6, 9], is a powerful concept, that like hypertext, offers users considerable benefits. In Ted's words:

> In this system, portions of content are brought in from various sources (local and remote). The content portions thus brought in may remain visibly connected to their origins. This is an important case of transclusion, which we define as the same content knowably in more than one place (For instance, being able to see a quotation or excerpt and its original context in another document.) [8]

Yet, like the term hypertext, the basic concept of transclusion is today so commonly encountered (implicitly, mainly via the web) that it has become as inconspicuous as electricity, or the inner workings of internal combustion engines. As advantageous as inconspicuousness can be (after all, who maintains their own car these days?), this "out-of-sight, out-of-mind" quality of transclusion has an unfortunate flip-side: not thinking much about it leads to not fully appreciating its future potential as much as we might, if only we thought about it more.

The purpose of this note is to make a rapid fly-by of the concept of transclusion, in order to expound opportunities for further capitalizing on its potential.

R.M. Akscyn (✉)
Knowledge Systems, Las Vegas NV 89135, USA
e-mail: rakscyn@gmail.com

© The Author(s) 2015   113
D.R. Dechow, D.C. Struppa (eds.), *Intertwingled*, History of Computing,
DOI 10.1007/978-3-319-16925-5_15

15.2   Background

My experience with the concept of transclusion comes mainly from the development of a series of hypertext systems over the past 36 years, beginning with a project in the Computer Science Department at Carnegie-Mellon University in 1978. Those systems were ZOG (CMU 1978–1985) [10], KMS (Knowledge Systems 1981–2006) [1], and Expeditee (University of Waikato 2006–2014) [2].

All three of these systems have transclusion at their core. This is done primarily by chunking the components of an artifact, such as a document or program, into screen-sized portions (called *frames*). Each frame then has a unique name so that it can be referenced by linking.

As a result, incorporating existing material into yet another artifact is merely a matter of creating a link to the existing frame representing the "top of the world" for that material. In general, the interpretation of such links is left to the devices of the link source side so that different treatments of the one-and-the-same transcluded material can be specified in multiple, independent-of-the-source ways.

15.3   Omitting Needless Features

Central to the design philosophy for these systems is simplicity. The primary approach to 'keeping it simple' has been to find data model, user interface and programming concepts that are not necessary for the sake of knowledge work—and then, to the extent practical, get rid of them. Thus, ironically, the ZOG/KMS/ Expeditee systems are defined as much by what they're not, as by what they are.

15.3.1   Data Model Omissions

The following concepts are omitted in the Expeditee conceptual data model:

Desktop, Dialogue Boxes, Files, Folders, Layers, Menu bars

In short, the functionality of all container types is provided by a single concept, the concept of a frame. A frame is a named, screen-sized graphics space, capable of containing any spatial arrangement of text, graphics, images, and sound objects (including overlapping) that users wish.

15.3.2   User Interface Omissions

The following concepts are omitted in the Expeditee user interface:

- Dialog Boxes
- Editors (there is no separate editing mode)

- Focus (focus always follow cursor position)
- Icons
- Menus (no menu bars, pull-down/pop-up menus)
- Naming (names are system-generated)
- Saving (saving is navigation-triggered)
- Scrolling
- Selection operation (operand scope is defaulted to whole items)
- Text cursor (no explicit focus representation)
- User interface (widget-ish objects are merely contents like any other)

Some central aspects of the Expeditee user interface are:

- All methods for existing objects (move, copy, delete, scale) are identical across all object types.
- All methods are single point-and-click (there are no conventional widgets).
- Execution time for methods is one second on average.
- System response time is one-twentieth of a second on average.
- Rate of interaction is typically hundreds of atomic methods per hour.

15.3.3   Programming Language Omissions

Some of the programming concepts omitted in the Expeditee scripting language are:

- Call-by-value
- Classes (and objects, as well as over a hundred other concepts of object-oriented programming)
- Declarations (variables are self-typing)
- Functions (there are only procedures)
- Global variables (all variables are local to their parent procedure)
- Goto (all transfers of control are calls-with-return)
- Keywords (no reserved terms)
- Programs (there is no program level, execution can begin at any block)
- Punctuation (commas, semi-colons, parentheses, braces)
- Symbol-controlled calling (all calls are done by links)
- User-defined data types (all data types—including images—are system-provided)

The only programming concepts in the ZOG/KMS/Expeditee trajectory are statements, variables, and "blocks" (as in "block- structured" languages), with some blocks being procedures with parameters. Since scripts—which are also represented in frames—can be associated with any object, virtually all programmatic function-ality occurs via stateless widgets, whereby all content types (points, lines, polygons, text, images) are "clickable" for the sake of invoking functionality.

15.3.4 Results of Omissions Trajectory

In short, the over-40 years of ZOG/KMS/Expeditee trajectory has been an embarrassingly slow "de-learning" of many of the concepts computer science has used to advance the state of the art over the past five decades. Thus, from the outside, these systems appear as though little or nothing has been developed, which is precisely what was intended so that, akin to a car windshield, users are rarely aware they are using a system. Instead, they are able to keep their attention on the task at hand.

On the other hand, there are some benefits that stem from using direct manipulation with spatial hypermedia to represent knowledge however one wishes: using scripts to post-process the user's representation, for example; and exporting contents to whatever formats downstream applications require.

To offer just one example, software development can be done in which the code is written in a personal programming dialect (which gets translated when exported) within a lattice of frames, each of which may contain whatever graphics, images, sounds, and colors the programmer wishes to collage along with the code (e.g., for comments by self or colleagues, links to related materials). Frames can transclude other frames that serve as layers overlaying widget collections as user interfaces, even on a frame-by-frame basis, so individual users can customize interaction functionality however suits them best. Note that coding inside a holistic environment that one can use for virtually all other knowledge development purposes is highly-unconventional relative to existing development environments and practices.

Ironically, much of what is actually done in such a hypertext-transclusion world—to expedite the production of knowledge artifacts—can't be done at all in most systems of today.

15.4 The Value of Transclusion

As alluded to above, transclusion is used in many systems, including virtually all hypertext systems [3, 4]. This section addresses a number of issues about transclusion such as examples, benefits, costs, trade offs, and opportunities for expanding the functionality of the concept beyond mere inclusion of original material. Existing examples of transclusion include:

- Images, scripts, and style sheets for web pages (invariably these are not in the base page of the webpage)
- Include files (and/or classes) for programs
- Layers in graphics programs
- Components stored in and dynamically accessible from a database (many web pages are database-based)

15.4.1 Benefits and Costs of Transclusion

The principal benefits of transclusion are reuse of existing material (versus re-inventing the wheel), and currency (access to the latest, greatest version of mate-rial). The principal costs of transclusion include finding desired/appropriate transcludeable material (an instance of "the research problem"), as well as effecting the transclusion, which might involve subsetting existing material, or transforming the transcluded material. To the extent that such subsetting and transforming involves sophisticated knowledge (because the interface mechanisms are complex) the less attractive using transclusion will be.

Benefits of transclusion can also be viewed through a cost-reduction lens, in the sense that transcluding existing material obviates having to create a facsimile from scratch. This principle is central, since, as in many things in life, if the cost of doing something is high, it often isn't done for lack of available time and money resources. In the case of software, the costs of re-developing components that are already stress-tested by time can be extreme (assuming we wish the same quality). Thus transclusion offers the benefits of creating artifacts that otherwise wouldn't be done.

Naturally there is a trade-off between benefits and costs constantly in play—since for material that is small (especially material that is static like prose in pub-lished papers)—retyping prose to serve as a quotation will often be far more efficient than trancluding the text. Conversely, re-capitulating the LaTeX markup for a math-ematics equation seen in a publication is sufficiently onerous that one would dearly love to transclude the original markup (even if that requires some work), if only such representations were generally available!

Thus simply transcluding the markup text shown in Fig. 15.1 from the author's original to directly achieve the same-as-original-author result shown in Fig. 15.2 would be a valuable expedient for reusing previous results, just as is the reuse of well-worn code.

```
\begin{equation}
    \label{IteratedFunctionSystem}
    R(h,q) =
        \begin{cases}
            0, & \text{if $h < q$} \\
            (h - 1) - \displaystyle\sum_{2 \leq p < q}
            \left ( R(\frac{h}{p}, p) + 1 \right ), & \text{otherwise}
        \end{cases}
\end{equation}
```

Fig. 15.1 LaTeX markup that produces Fig. 15.1

$$R(h,q) = \begin{cases} 0, & \text{if } h < q \\ (h-1) - \sum_{2 \le p < q} \left(R(\frac{h}{p},p) + 1 \right), & \text{otherwise} \end{cases}$$

Fig. 15.2 Visually complex mathematical equation generated from transcluded LaTeX markup

15.4.2 How Can Opportunities for Transclusion Be Expanded?

Opportunities for transclusion can be expanded via several dimensions:

- Expanding the sources of accessible material that is permissibly transcludable (i.e., does not violate copyright as well as generally accepted norms)
- Expanding the set of transformations that can be performed on the transcluded material
- Decreasing the size of the smallest grain size of transcludeable material
- Making transclusions recursive

15.4.3 Expanding the Source of Accessible Material

Naturally having more to choose from is better than having less. But such a capability is meaningless if the inconvenience of finding and collecting candidates, for repeated side-by-side comparison, is too high. As the saying goes, "In theory, theory is sufficient; in practice it isn't." Thus, the efficiency of every step of the transclusion ecosystem is critical to the degree transcludable material will be used.

Factors such as how well collections of material are organized will likely dramatically affect what actually happens, no matter the richness of the possibilities. Indeed, building on the well-known expression:

If it isn't written, it doesn't exist.

We might add:

If it's not in the library, it doesn't exist. (and)
If it's in the library, but is too hard to find, it doesn't exist.

But in addition to accessibility is the issue of just what can be done with transcludable material. Since the purpose of most knowledge artifacts is to contribute something original, simply reusing existing material, as is, may not provide value sufficient for the task at hand. Thus expanding the set of transformations that can be performed on the transcluded material beyond exact copying—is a way of expanding the design space for transclusion. This in turn admits for higher 'value' peaks that greatly increase the ROI of effort invested.

But in addition to accessibility is the issue of just what can be done with transcludable material. Since the purpose of most knowledge artifacts is to contribute something original, simply reusing existing material, as is, may not provide value sufficient for the task at hand. Thus expanding the set of transformations that can be performed on the transcluded material beyond exact copying—is a way of expanding the design space for transclusion. This in turn allows for higher 'value peaks' that greatly increase the ROI of effort invested.

15.4.4 What Are the Types of Transformation of Transclusions?

Some easily-envisioned transformations of material include:

- Subsetting (e.g., clipping out just a portion of a source image) results in more flexibility to get just the portion you need for the purpose you are striving to attain
- Scaling (up or down, through a wide-range of size increments)
- Re-colorizing (e.g., taking a greyscale image and displaying it using any base color)
- Rotation (e.g., any of the 360°)
- Associating a script to be activated when users interact with the displayed transclusion

One could, for example, create an artistic rendering of a Christmas tree, one with the decorative balls all being the same size and color. But the result might not be as engaging as a smattering of such ornaments with a variety of colors and sizes with all the different renditions transcluded and transformed from a single source image.

More sophisticated transformations might include:

- Translation of prose from one language to another
- Animation by 'tweening' between two different states (of the same scene)
- Speeding up the rate of animation of a GIF image
- Overlaying multiple animations on top of one another

In short, the ability to specify transformations as part of the transclusion reference, turns the source material into an abstraction—one whose generality spans all the combinations of the transformation dimensions. Thus, for example, size (say 50 settings), color (100 settings), and rotation (360 settings) by themselves would provide over 1.5 million possible variations of a single object.

15.4.5 Decreasing the Grain Size Directly Transcludable

Another dimension of expanding the design space is decreasing the grain size of what is directly trancludable—as a way of obviating the cost of purpose-built mechanisms that (in theory) can do the job—but at prohibitive cost. An underlying motivation for this dimension is that components can only be so big, because at the limit you're simply regurgitating the original message. It will always be better to be able to use just the right-sized building block for the purpose at hand, e.g., only part of an image, text, or code.

Take the example of re-using the LaTeX code for a mathematical expression that was shown in Fig. 15.1 and 15.2. The reuse was significantly streamlined by the fact that the mark-up text in question is in an Expeditee frame of its own (from one of my math papers). As a result, trancluding it in this book chapter, only required copying its title (which in Expeditee auto-links to the frame where it resides) and plunking that linked item down in the relevant frame of the set I'm using to author this chapter. Two such transclusions were made—both to the one-and-only frame—one transclusion for showing the verbatim LaTeX source (Fig. 15.1) and the other to be interpreted by LaTeX to show the graphical end result (Fig. 15.2) it specifies.

By comparison, transcluding such an equation out of a whole-document text file would require significant work—to denote the beginning and ending character positions of the text within the file or, alternatively, cropping a portion of a screenshot. While conceivably the original author might have placed the equation within a file of its own, that's not common practice. Thus in addition to the fact that such upsteam-of-WYSIWIG files are generally not publically-accessible to begin with, the hassle of figuring out how to effect the transclusion would likely deter all but the most persevering of re-users. Indeed, many applications can't even transclude their own handiwork, even from artifacts created by the same user on the same system.

This particular example was chosen because it also illustrates the previous point about transformations, for it is the same Expeditee frame that is transcluded both times: first for the sake of showing the underlying LaTeX code, and then again for the sake of generating the end-view as seen in the original paper. The ability to have "the same content knowably in more than one place," but with a different presentation each time, is a good example of how separating presentation properties from content is a powerful mechanism for reuse (i.e., by avoiding embedded markup, as Ted has argued for decades [7]).

15.4.6 *Making Transclusions Recursive*

Finally, making the transclusions themselves be constellations of transcludable material further adds to the panoply of material that users can selectively reuse.

15.5 Conclusions

In summary, here are some take-home messages about transclusion:

- Since the fastest way to do something is to not have to do it at all, the ability to reuse an existing, well-crafted, extensively-tested existing artifact (or portion thereof) is one way to avoid having to spend time and money developing that component.

- Transclusion offers a powerful mechanism for reusing material and thus expanding the volume of material that can be created over time. Such volume is critical to the creation of high value, as it better allows for authors to add value by giving us the best of a lot (which is a lot better than the best of a little).

- Potential reuse of transcludable material is greatly expanded if the mechanism for effecting the transcluding can also transform the original in desired ways, such as subsetting (cropping out portions of images as well as text), scaling, colorizing, and other desired transformations–including forming aggregates in which the same original is collaged in multiple, independent ways. Thus the ability to transform transcludable material within a large design space makes the original material inherently more reusable.

- Potential reuse of transcludable material is further fostered by the ability of transcluded material to contain transclusions of their own. In other words, by having the concept be fully recursive. This enables repositories of transcludable material to themselves be multi-level–enabling users to simply tap into whatever level of aggregation suits their creative purpose (e.g., from individual Christmas tree ornament, to the whole tree, on up to an entire landscape).

- But *potential* reuse is not the same as *practical* reuse. Thus, mechanisms for finding and transcluding material need to be efficient, as generally speaking whatever is inefficient is done much less often and therefore is not as valuable in practice as it sounds in theory.

- A recommendation: the more developers might collaborate to create common models of transclusion, as opposed to the endless one-upmanship now practiced—the more transclusion can come out of the closet, and be seen as a core capability that helps all knowledge workers lift their game across all their work, creating greater value for their organizations and clients.

References

1. Akscyn RM, McCracken DL, Yoder EA (1988) KMS: a distributed hypermedia system for managing knowledge in organization. Commun ACM 31(7):820–835
2. Akscyn RM (2009) The expeditee project: measuring the productivity of knowledge work. In: Proceedings of the New Zealand computer science research students conference. Auckland University, New Zealand
3. Bernstein M (2003) Collage, composites, construction. In: Proceedings of the fourteenth ACM conference on hypertext and hypermedia. ACM, p 122
4. Krottmaier H, Maurer H (2001) Transclusions in the 21st century. J Univ Comput Sci 7(12):1125–1136

5. Nelson TH (1965) A file structure for the complex, the changing and the indeterminate. In: Proceedings of the ACM 20th national conference, pp 84–100
6. Nelson TH (1995) The heart of connection: hypermedia unified transclusion. Commun ACM 38(8):31–33
7. Nelson TH (1997) Embedded markup considered harmful. In XML: principles, tools and techniques. World Wide Web J 2(4):129–134. Sebastopol: O'Reilly. http://www.xml.com/lpt/a/294
8. Nelson TH (2007) Toward a deep electronic literature: the generalization of documents and media. Project Xanadu. http://xanadu.com/XanaduSpace/xuGzn.htm. Accessed 16 Dec 2014
9. Nelson TH, Smith RA, Mallicoat M (2007) Back to the future: hypertext the way it used to be. In: Proceedings of the eighteenth ACM conference on hypertext & hypermedia, pp 227–228
10. Newell A, McCracken D, Robertson G, Akscyn R (1981) ZOG and the USS Carl Vinson. In: Computer science research review. Camegie-Mellon University, pp 95–118

Chapter 16
Ted Nelson: A Critical (and Critically Incomplete) Bibliography

Henry Lowood

16.1 Introduction

Devoting time to serious bibliographical matters as a tribute to Ted Nelson may seem like a quaintly out-of-tune and bookish, if not totally misguided project. It is easy to pigeon-hole Ted's work as belonging to a generation of adventurous and creative writers and editors active during the 1960s who began to find that traditional print media constrained the expression of their ideas. Marshall McLuhan and the *Whole Earth Catalog* come to mind. Indeed, *Literary Machines* opens with the declaration that it is "a hypertext, or nonsequential piece of writing." Each reader of this book has confronted the difficulties imposed by non-linear writing on the linear medium of print.

And yet, there is no way around the fact that most of Ted's work has been published on paper. This fact alone does not produce a particularly difficult problem for bibliography. The difficulty is rather that many of his important writings appeared in ephemeral or semi-published formats, ranging from conference proceedings and magazines of every ilk to self-published books that were produced anywhere and nowhere – at least from the perspective of libraries such as my own that tried desperately to acquire copies. As a result of the vagabond nature of the Nelson oeuvre, few libraries own more than a few of his published works, and several of his most important texts, such as the earliest editions of *Computer Lib/Dream Machines* and *Literary Machines* have achieved almost legendary status for being difficult to lay hands on. So where are we to turn for the texts?

Thus, this bibliography. At least it is a start. My goal has been to put together a complete picture of Ted Nelson's body of work as expressed in publication, including selections from ephemeral and non-print media. It has not been easy. As the

H. Lowood (✉)
Stanford University Libraries, Stanford, CA, USA
e-mail: lowood@stanford.edu

© The Author(s) 2015
D.R. Dechow, D.C. Struppa (eds.), *Intertwingled*, History of Computing,
DOI 10.1007/978-3-319-16925-5_16

former bibliographer of the Society for the History of Technology, I adopted and long held to the habit of requiring visual inspection of texts that appeared in my bibliographies. Until this project, I had little reason to abandon this practice. Academic publication practices are easy to trace. It turns out that a number of Ted's publications have followed different paths to readers. Since they have often eluded library catalogs and on-line databases, I have had to trust sources such as c.v. entries, footnotes, and Web traces more than I would like. As a compromise with my earlier bibliographic rule, I have included most of what I have found, indicating works that I was unable to inspect with an asterisk preceding their entries in this bibliography. I ask that any readers who may have access to these texts to contact me. I will produce a revised version of this bibliography someday, if revisions are necessary as a result from any such contacts. Ted's work is worth it.

Theodor H. Nelson Bibliography

*Nelson TH, Caplan RL (1957) Anything & everything: the 1957 Hamburg show at Swarthmore College. Audio recording – 33 1/3 rpm microgroove, Swarthmore

Nelson TH (1958) Schematics, systematics, normatics. http://tprints.ecs.soton.ac.uk/4/

Nelson TH (1959) The Epiphany of Slocum Furlow. https://www.youtube.com/watch?v=rFguI6rwNbQ. Student film, Streamed video uploaded 2012.

*Nelson TH (1959) We need a sociology department. Swarthmore, PA. Collected essays written as an undergraduate at Swarthmore College

Nelson TH (1965) A file structure for the complex, the changing and the indeterminate. In: ACM '65: proceedings of the 20th national conference. Association for Computing Machinery, New York, pp 84–100. doi:10.1145/800197.806036. Paper 4.2 prepared for session 4, "Complex Information Processing," of the 1965 ACM Conference. Reprinted, with introduction by Noah Wardrip-Fruin. In: eds. Noah Wardrip-Fruin and Nick Montfort (eds) The new media reader. Cambridge: MIT Press, 2003, pp 133–45

Nelson TH (1965) Computer-indexed film handling. J SMPTE – Soc Motion Pict Telev Eng 74:818–819. (Preprint of conference presentation)

*Nelson TH (1965) Suggestion for an on-line Braille display. In: Proceedings of the society for information display. Society for Information Display. Paper presented to Sixth National Symposium on Information Display, Los Angeles, pp 31–39

*Nelson TH (1965) The hypertext. In: Proceedings of the World Documentation Federation

Nelson TH (1966–1967) Hypertext notes. http://web.archive.org/web/20031127035740/http://www.xanadu.com/XUarchive/. Unpublished series of ten short essays or "notes"

Nelson TH (1967) Getting it out of our system. In: Schechter G (ed) Information retrieval: a critical review. Thompson Books, Washington, DC, pp 191–210

Nelson TH, Carmody S, Gross W, Rice D, van Dam A (1969) A hypertext editing system for the/360. In: Faiman M, Nievergelt J (eds) Pertinent concepts in computer graphics. Proceedings of the Second University of Illinois conference on computer graphics. University of Illinois Press, Urbana, pp 291–330

Nelson TH (1970) Las Vegas confrontation sit-out: a CAI radical's view from solitary. ACM SIGCUE Outlook, October, 12–15. doi: 10.1145/965768.965770. "This is an account of a round-table discussion on computer contributions to curriculum which I chaired, or perhaps charred, at the Fall Joint Computer Conference, 1969. It was a mortifying experience: everyone walked out. Herewith my dutiful report"

Nelson TH (1970) Barnum-Tronics. Swarthmore Colleg Alumni Bull 12–15

Nelson TH (1970) The crafting of media. http://xanadu.com.au/ted/TN/PUBS/CraftMedia.html. "A short piece about the future design of electronic media, as I was thinking from 1960 to 1970"

Nelson TH (1970) No more teachers dirty looks. Comput Decis September, 16–23 (Reprinted in Dream Machines (1974), 16–19, and, with introduction by Noah Wardrip-Fruin, In: The new media reader, Wardrip-Fruin N, Montfort N (eds) MIT Press, Cambridge, 2003, pp 308–316)

Nelson TH (1971) Computopia and cybercrud. In: Levien RE (ed) Computers in instruction: their future for higher education: proceedings of a conference held in October 1970. A Report Prepared for National Science Foundation and Carnegie Commission on Higher Education, pp 185–99. R-718-NSF/CCOM/RC. Santa Monica, CA; Washington, D.C.: The RAND Corporation; distributed by ERIC Clearinghouse. http://files.eric.ed.gov/fulltext/ED052635.pdf

*Nelson TH (1971) The route to Halftone image synthesis. Comput Decis May. Begins p. 12

Nelson TH (1973) A conceptual framework for man-machine everything. In: Proceedings of the June 4–8, 1973, National Computer Conference and Exposition, m21–26. AFIPS '73. ACM, New York. doi:10.1145/1499586.1499776

*Nelson TH (1973) As we will think. In: Online 72: conference proceedings … International conference on online interactive computing, Brunel University, Uxbridge, 4–7 September 1972, pp 439–54. Uxbridge, England: Online Computer Systems, Ltd. Examines Vannevar's Bush 1945 essay. Reprinted In: James M. Nyce and Paul Kahn (eds) From memex to hypertext: Vannevar Bush and the mind's machine. Academic Press, Boston, 1991, pp 245–260

Nelson TH (1974) Computer Lib: you can and must understand computers now/dream machines: new freedoms through computer screens – a minority report. Chicago: Hugo's Book Service, for the author. Two books joined together in tête-bêche format. A reprint edition was created from negatives in 2013 by the author

Nelson TH, DeFanti TA, Sandin DJ (1975) Computer graphics as a way of life. Comput Gr 1(1):9–15. doi:10.1016/0097-8493(75)90026-6. Originally presented at the first SIGGRAPH Conference, 1974, with abstract published in SIGGRAPH '74 proceedings of the 1st annual conference on computer graphics and interactive techniques. ACM, New York, 1974, 4.

*Nelson TH (1975) Data realms and magic windows. In: ACPA-5: papers presented at the 5th conference – association of computer programmers and analysts

*Nelson TH (1976) [Television]. Chicago, January, 106. Untitled contribution to section called "Television," originally submitted under the title "Explorable Screens"

Nelson TH (1977) The home computer revolution. In: Nelson TH (ed) South Bend, Ind.; distributed by the Distributors

Nelson TH (1977) A dream for Irving Snerd. Creat Comput May–June, 79–81. Xanadu introduced in cartoon format. (Reprinted in The best of creative computing, vol. 3 (1980), 24–26)

Nelson TH (1977) PCC interviews Ted Nelson. People's Computer Company, February 5(4):41

Nelson TH (1977) Those unforgettable next two years. In: The first west coast computer faire: a conference & exposition on personal & home computers, 15–17 April 1977, San Francisco. conference proceedings. Computer Faire, Palo Alto, 20–25

Nelson TH (1978) Electronic publishing and electronic literature. In: DeLand EC (ed) Information technology in health science education. Plenum Medical, New York, pp 211–216

*Nelson TH (1979) Next year in Xanadu. Swarthmore, PA. Audio recording

Nelson TH (1980) ホームコンピュータ革命. Sotec, Inc., Tokyo. Translation of Home Computer Revolution by Nishi Jun'ichirō

Nelson TH (1980) Actors 2. The story continues (= "Symposium on Actor Languages", part 2). Creat Comput 6(11):73–94. (Edited collection of articles, with contributions by Nelson)

Nelson TH (1980) Interactive systems and the design of virtuality. Creat Comput 6(11):56–62; (12):94–106

Nelson TH (1980) John Mauchly, 1907–1980. Creat Comput 6(3) March, 8. (A "personal reminiscence")

Nelson TH (1980) Replacing the printed word: a complete literary system. In: Information processing 80: proceedings of IFIP Congress 80: Tokyo, Japan October 6–9, 1980, Melbourne, Australia October 14–17, 1980, 1013–23. IFIP Congress Series 8. North-Holland Publishing, Amsterdam

Nelson TH (1980) Symposium on actor languages. Creat Comput 6(10):61–86 (edited collection of articles, with contributions by Nelson)

Nelson TH (1980) The Atari machine. Creat Comput 6(6):34–35

Nelson TH (1981) Literary machines: the report on, and of, project Xanadu concerning word processing, electronic publishing, hypertext, thinkertoys, tomorrows intellectual revolution, and certain other topics including knowledge, education and freedom. Theodor H. Nelson, Swarthmore (Subsequent re-publication dates appear to be: 1981, 1982, 1983, 1984, 1987, 1990, 1991, 1992 and 1993. The 1987 publication was a revision (version 87.1), as was the version published in 1992 and 1993 (version 93.1). Only the 1981, 1987, 1990, 1992 and 1993 publications could be verified against privately or institutionally held copies)

Nelson TH (1981) Mail Chauvinism: the magicians, the Snark and the Camel. Creat Comput 7(11):128–130, 134–138, 140–144, 150, 156. (Report on the Electronic mail and message conference)

Nelson TH (1982) A new home for the mind. Datamat, March, 169–180. Reprinted In: Mayer PA (ed) Computer media and communication: a reader. Oxford University Press, Oxford 2000

Nelson TH (1982) Smoothers of the lost arc. Creat Comput 8(3):86–110. Report describing the 1981 SIGGRAPH meeting

*Nelson TH (1982) Why computer ease is so difficult. In: Proceedings of control data software design conference, October 1982

Nelson TH (1983) The electronic office: how simple can you get? OAC'83 Conference Digest. The Fourth Annual Office Automation Conference, 9–15

Nelson TH (1984) Computopia now! In: Digital deli: the comprehensive, user-lovable menu of computer lore, culture, lifestyles, and fancy. Workman Publishing, New York, pp 349–351

Nelson TH (1986) A technical overview of the Xanadu electronic storage and publishing system. VHS. [San Antonio, TX]: Project Xanadu. VHS

*Nelson TH (1986) A vision of the future. Publishers Weekly, November 23

Nelson TH (1986) The posterity machine. VHS. [San Antonio, TX]: Project Xanadu. VHS. Lecture at Vassar College, 1986

Nelson TH (1986c) The tyranny of the file. Datamat 32(24):83–86

Nelson TH (1987) All for one and one for all. In: Hypertext '87: proceedings of the ACM conference on hypertext. HYPERTEXT '87. ACM, New York. pp v–vii. doi:10.1145/317426.317427

Nelson TH (1987) Computer lib …/dream machines … Tempus Books of Microsoft Press, Redmond, Revised and updated edition

Nelson TH (1987) Literary machines … Edition 87.1. South Bend, Ind.: The Distributors. http://archive.org/details/Literary.Machines.1987 ("Literary Machines, published by the author, 1981; various revisions from year to year; this is edition 87.1, being published by the author, 1987. Simultaneous mass-market edition being published by special arrangement by The Distributors, 702 South Michigan, South Bend IN 46618; simultaneous Macintosh hypertext edition in GUIDE being published by Owl International, Inc., 14218 NE 21st Street, Bellevue WA 98007")

*Nelson TH (1987) The checkmate proposal. ("Circulated as printout")

Nelson TH (1988a) Managing immense storage. Byte 13(1):225–238

*Nelson TH (1988) The call of the ocean: hypertext universal and open. Hyperage, May–June, 5–7

Nelson TH (1988b) Unifying tomorrow's hypermedia. In: Online information 88. 12th international online information meeting, vol 1. Learned Information, Oxford, pp 1–7

Nelson TH (1989) Hyperwelcome. Hypermedia 1(1):3–5. http://dl.acm.org/citation.cfm?id=66840

*Nelson TH (1990) How hypertext (Un)does the Canon. Modern Language Association, Chicago (Usually cited by this title. Title given as "How Xanadu (Un) does the Canon" in the MLA Session Announcement published in Postmodern Culture 1, no. 1 (Sept. 1990))

Nelson TH (1990) Literary machines … 89.1 edn. Mindful Press, Sausalito

Nelson TH (1990) On the Xanadu project. Byte, September, 298–299. Contribution to "Welcome to the Byte Summit: Sixty-three of the Most Creative and Influential People in the Industry Discuss Their Perspectives on the Microcomputer Industry of the Future"

Nelson TH (1990) The once and future literature. J Inf Sci 16(6):339–43. http://jis.sagepub.com/content/16/6/339.short

Nelson TH (1990d) The right way to think about software design. In: The art of human-computer interface design. Addison-Wesley, Reading, pp 235–243

Nelson TH (1990) Virtual world without end. In: Proceedings of cyber arts international conference, September 1990. Keynote address published separately as Virtual World Without End. Mindful Press, Sausalito, 1990?

*Nelson TH, Jul E (1991) Theodor Nelson describes Xanadu: worldwide hypertext publishing. OCLC Newsletter, no. 194

Nelson TH (1992) Literary Machines … 93.1 edn. Mindful Press, Sausalito

Nelson TH (1992) Literary Machines … 93.1 edn. Mindful Press, Sausalito. (Electronic hypertext edition distributed by Eastgate Systems)

Nelson TH (1992) Literary machines 90.1: Il Projetto Xanadu. Padova: Muzzio. Translation of Literary Machines 90.1 into Italian

Nelson TH (1992d) Opening hypertext: a memoir. In: Tuman MC (ed) Literacy online, the promise (and Peril) of reading and writing with computers, Pittsburgh series in composition, literacy, and culture. University of Pittsburgh Press, Pittsburgh, pp 43–57

Nelson TH (1992) Silicon valley story, the preview 1.3. https://www.youtube.com/watch?v=AXlyMrv8_dQ Excerpt (?) of "The Silicon Valley Show" uploaded in 2010 to YouTube

Nelson TH (1992) The silicon valley show. http://archive.org/details/Timothy_Leary_Archives_189.dv. A video short called "The Silicon Valley Show" featuring Ted Nelson, Douglas Engelbart, Rick Mascitti, Stewart Brand, and Timothy Leary. Directed by Ted Nelson

Nelson TH (1992) Xanadu space, 1993. Autodesk, Sausalito. http://archive.org/details/01Kahle000838. Wide Area Information Servers Project Documentation, scanned in 2013

Nelson TH (1993) Literary Machines … 93.1 edn. Mindful Press, Sausalito, CA

Nelson TH (1993) Publishing contracts for a point-and-click Universe. Xanadu World Publishing Repository, Sausalito. http://archive.org/details/01Kahle000846. Wide Area Information Servers Project Documentation, scanned in 2013

Nelson TH (1993) The secret of human life. J Econ Soc Intell 3(2):84–94. http://tprints.ecs.soton.ac.uk/5/. Adapted from manuscript draft of an as yet unpublished book, Biostrategy and Polymind. An article draft under the title, "The Secret of Human Life: A revisionist view of human psychology and evolution from the book in progress, Biostrategy and Polymind: A New Theory of Human Life," dated 8 Oct. 1987, is available here: http://tprints.ecs.soton.ac.uk/5/1/seclife.txt

Nelson TH (1993) World enough: the manuscript edition. Mindful Press, Sausalito. http://archives.obs-us.com/obs/english/papers/ted/tedtoc1.htm. Autobiographical texts "under negotiation for serialization, and publishing this limited edition is part of that negotiation"

Nelson TH (1993) You will, Oscar, you will!: the implications of free quotability and transpublication. Xanadu World Publishing Repository, Sausalito. http://archive.org/details/01Kahle000829. Wide Area Information Servers Project Documentation, scanned in 2013. Summary of address to the Annual Meeting of the Association of American University Presses, Salt Lake City, June 1993

Nelson TH (1994) リテラリーマシン: ハイパーテキスト原論. Tokyo: ASCII Corporation. Translation of Literary Machines 91.1 by Ikuo Takeuchi and Saito Yasushionore

Nelson TH (1994b) A publishing and royalty model for networked documents. In: IMA intellectual property project proceedings, vol 1. Interactive Multimedia Association, Annapolis, pp 257–259

Nelson TH (1994) Xanadu: document interconnection enabling re-use with automatic author credit and royalty accounting. Inf Serv Use 14(4):255–265. http://iospress.metapress.com/index/MH27753662736246.pdf

Nelson TH (1994) Xanadu publishing with royalty: 1994 One BBSCON. [S.l.]: PlaybackNow.com. Audio recording of lecture by Ted Nelson at the ONE BBSCON in August 1994 concerning his ideas for handling rights management in electronic publishing

Nelson TH (1995) The heart of connection: hypermedia unified by transclusion. Commun ACM 38(8):31–33. doi:10.1145/208344.208353

Nelson TH (1996) Issues in applicative hyperization of unwitting systems. In: ACM proceedings of the second international workshop on incorporating hypertext functionality into software systems, 1996. http://web.archive.org/web/20000613061623/http://www.cs.nott.ac.uk/~hla/HTF/HTFII/Nelson.html. Paper delivered to HTF II – The Second International Workshop on Incorporating Hypertext Functionality Into Software Systems

Nelson TH (1997a) Crush and crash: logic of a terrible tomorrow. Commun ACM 40(2):90–91. doi:10.1145/253671.253729

Nelson TH (1997) Embedded markup considered harmful. In: XML: principles, tools and techniques, 2(4), Fall, 129–134. World Wide Web Journal, O'Reilly, Sebastopol. http://www.xml.com/lpt/a/294 or http://www.xml.com/pub/a/w3j/s3.nelson.html

Nelson TH (1997) Literature to last: design for a universal digital medium. In: Hagel U (ed) Labile Ordnungen: Netze Denken, Kunst Verkehren, Verbindlichkeiten. Interface 3. Hamburg: Hans-Bredow-Institut für Rundfunk und Fernsehen, pp 98–102

Nelson TH (1997d) The future of information: ideas, connections and the gods of electronic literature. ASCII Corporation, Tokyo

Nelson TH (1997) Transcopyright: a simple legal arrangement for sharing, re-use and republication of copyrighted material on the net. In: Worldwide computing and its applications. International conference, WWCA'97. Proceedings. Lecture notes in computer science 1274. Springer, Berlin/New York, pp 7–14. http://link.springer.com/content/pdf/10.1007/3-540-63343-X_34.pdf

Nelson TH (1997) Transcopyright: dealing with the dilemma of digital copyright. Educom Rev 32(1):32–35. http://eric.ed.gov/?id=EJ536232. "Cleanup" of Draft dated 14 Oct. 1998 available under the title, "Transcopyright: Pre-Permission for Virtual Republishing" at: http://www.xanadu.com.au/ted/transcopyright/transcopy.html

Nelson TH (1998) What's on my mind. In: Invited talk at the first wearable computer conference. Fairfax VA. http://xanadu.com.au/ted/zigzag/xybrap.html. Written version of paper delivered to first Wearable computer conference

Nelson TH (1998) Xanadu ZigZag hyperstructure kit: ZigZag commands for version 0.49. http://www.xanadu.com/zigzag/zzDirex.html. "System designed by Ted Nelson, programmed by Andrew Pam. These instructions by TN"

Nelson TH (1999) The unfinished revolution and Xanadu. ACM Comput Surv 31(4es), December, article 37. doi:10.1145/345966.346039

Nelson TH (1999) Time to liberate the web. Inter@ctive Week, October 25

Nelson TH (1999) Way out of the box. October 8. http://ted.hyperland.com/TQdox/zifty.d9-TQframer.html

Nelson TH (1999) Xanalogical structure, needed now more than ever: parallel documents, deep links to content, deep versioning, and deep re-use. ACM Comput Surv 31(4es), December, article 33, 1–32. doi:10.1145/345966.346033

Nelson TH (2000) Many-to-many payments system for network content materials. http://www.google.com/patents/US6058381. US Patent 08/961,570, application dated 30 Oct 1997

Nelson TH (2001) Ted Nelson at ACM hypertext 2001 Streamed video. http://vimeo.com/15593138

Nelson TH (2001) Interactive connection, viewing and maneuvering system for complex data. http://www.google.com/patents/US6262736. US Patent application 09/530,857, application dated 15 Nov 1998

Nelson TH (2001) The future of information (scanned). May 4. http://web.archive.org/web/20010504071817/http://www.xanadu.com.au/ted/INFUTscans/INFUTscans.html

Nelson TH (2001) Xanadu technologies – an introduction, 4 October." http://xanadu.com/tech/ (A Joint Disclosure by Udanax.com and Project Xanadu as of August 23, 1999 to accompany our presentation at the O'Reilly Open Source Conference. … [Updated to reflect what was actually said at the meeting, with clarifications of the illustrations that were shown. Further citations will be found in our ACM paper in preparation, "Xanalogical Structure: Needed Now More Than Ever" at http://www.xanadu.com.au/ted/XUsurvey/xuDation.html. See also our book Literary Machines])

Nelson TH (2001) The ZigZag® database and visualization system: the true generalization of structure, 11 January. http://xanadu.com/zigzag/

Nelson TH (2001) Zigzag (Tech Briefing). In: Proceedings of the 12th ACM conference on hypertext and hypermedia. ACM, New York, pp 261–262. http://dl.acm.org/citation.cfm?id=504281

Nelson TH (2002) Philosophy of hypertext. PhD dissertation, Keio University

Nelson TH (2003) I don't buy in. March. http://ted.hyperland.com/buyin.txt

Nelson TH (2003) Structure, tradition and possibility. In: Hypertext 03: the fourteenth ACM conference on hypertext and hypermedia, August 26–30, 2003, Nottingham, UK, 1. ACM, New York. doi:10.1145/900051.900053

Nelson TH (2004) A cosmology for a different computer universe: data model, mechanisms, virtual machine and visualization infrastructure. J Digit Inf 5(1). https://journals.tdl.org/jodi/index.php/jodi/article/view/131/129

Nelson TH (2004) The world wide web at 10: the dream and the reality. Rose-Hulman Institute of Technology, Terre Haute, Audio recording of conference presentations

Nelson TH (2005) The politics of internet software: 'geeks bearing gifts.' Streamed video. http://webcast.oii.ox.ac.uk/?view=Webcast&ID=20051121_112. Oxford Internet Institute webcast

Nelson TH (2005) Transhyperability and Argumedia. New Rev Hypermed Multimed 11(1):27–32. doi:10.1080/13614560500202191. Invited commentary on D. Kolb, "Association and Argument: Hypertext In and Around the Writing Process," pp. 7–26 in this journal issue

Nelson TH (2005c) Translit (TM): the new open-source Xanadu. New Mag: Int Vis Verbal Commun 1:114–119

Nelson TH (2005) Transliterature™: a humanist format for re-usable documents and media – deep, open, re-user-friendly, free-form, nonhierarchical, profusely connectable, 22 October. http://transliterature.org/

Nelson TH (2006) It could all be so much better. New Sci 191(2569):54–55. http://www.science-direct.com/science/article/pii/S0262407906605046

Nelson TH (2006b) Lost in hyperspace. New Scientist 191(2561):26

Nelson TH, Smith RA (2007) Back to the future: hypertext the way it used to be. In: Proceedings of the eighteenth conference on hypertext and hypermedia. ACM, New York, pp 227–228. http://dl.acm.org/citation.cfm?id=1286303. Text available at http://xanadu.com/XanaduSpace/btf.htm.

Nelson TH (2007) Toward a deep electronic literature: the generalization of documents and media. April 4. http://xanadu.com/XanaduSpace/xuGzn.htm

Nelson TH (2007) Transclusion: fixing electronic literature. https://www.youtube.com/watch?v=Q9kAW8qeays. Streamed video of Google Tech Talk, 29 January

Nelson TH (2008) A very general lecture, Part 1. Streamed video. http://webcast.oii.ox.ac.uk/?view=Webcast&ID=20080317_236. Oxford Internet Institute webcast

Nelson TH (2008) Geeks bearing gifts: how the computer world got this way. V. 1.1. Mindful Press, Sausalito; distributed by Lulu.com. http://www.lulu.com/shop/ted-nelson/geeks-bearing-gifts/paperback/product-4312837.html

Nelson TH (2008) System for exploring connections between data pages. http://www.google.com/patents/US20090222717. U.S. Patent application 12/039,656, filed 28 Feb

Nelson TH (2010) Possiplex: movies, intellect, creative control, my computer life and the fight for civilization: an autobiography of Ted Nelson. Mindful Press, Hackettstown; distributed by Lulu.com. http://www.lulu.com/shop/ted-nelson/possiplex/ebook/product-17533977.html

Nelson TH (2011) Dr Ted Nelson – interwingularity: when ideas collide. Resource. July 5. http://
videos.southampton.ac.uk/80/   or   https://www.youtube.com/watch?v=EwPnOD8Qlpk.
Streamed video of seminar held in 2007, University of Southampton, as part of 70th Birthday
celebration
Nelson TH (2011) Ted Nelson on the future of text, Milde Norway, October 2011. Streamed video.
http://vimeo.com/31039323
Nelson TH (2012) Computers for cynics, May. Available via the TheTedNelson YouTube channel,
https://www.youtube.com/channel/UCr_DXJ7ZUAJO_d8CnHYTDMQ.   Streamed   video.
Eight-part series on topics in the history of computing
Nelson TH (2013) Future of text 2013: Ted Nelson. Streamed video. https://www.youtube.com/
watch?v=SCoivDX3DFY&feature=youtube_gdata_player.   From   the   Future   of   Text
Symposium at the London College of Communication, London, England, 2013
Nelson TH (2013) Ted Nelson at HomeBrew computer club reunion 11-11-13. Streamed video.
https://www.youtube.com/watch?v=rbqPqp9y_1Q. Lecture at HomeBrew Computer Club
reunion, 11 November, Computer History Museum
Nelson TH (2013) Ted Nelson's eulogy for Douglas Engelbart. Streamed video. https://www.you-
tube.com/watch?v=yMjPqr1s-cg. Given at the Computer History Museum in Mountain View,
California, on 9 December
Nelson TH (2014) Intertwingled: Ted Nelson, 'what box?.' Streamed video. http://ibc.chapman.
edu/Mediasite/Play/83d7b9016e3a42ecaf112cc4620e719f1d. Concluding talk of the conference, "Intertwingled: The Work and Influence of Ted Nelson," Chapman College, Orange, 24
April
Nelson TH (2014) Life, love, college, etc, 2nd edn. Mindful Press. http://www.lulu.com/shop/
theodor-holm-nelson/life-love-college-etc/paperback/product-21479799.html.   Collected
essays written for the Swarthmore Phoenix as an undergraduate. Originally compiled in 1959
with the alternate title We Need a Sociology Department, and possibly reprinted at Reed
College in 1992
Nelson TH (2014) The scene machine. Mindful Press, Sausalito; distributed by Lulu.com. http://
www.lulu.com/shop/theodor-holm-nelson/the-scene-machine/paperback/product-21454515.
html
Nelson TH (2014) Ted Nelson home page. http://ted.hyperland.com/. Accessed 19 Dec. Website
includes "Curriculum Vitae: Theodor Holm Nelson, Ph.D," http://hyperland.com/TNvita

Part IV
The Last Word

Chapter 17
What Box?

Theodor Holm Nelson

17.1 Introduction

Most people don't get to hear their obituaries. I feel very lucky to have eavesdropped
on these thoughtful pre-mortems, and I want to thank all the authors for their understanding, kindness, wit, and forbearance. I feel much better understood than I knew.

First let me thank several people: Daniele Struppa and Doug Dechow for the gift
of the event and this book; My son Erik and his mother Deborah Stone for their
understanding and great moral support over the years; and my collaborator, ex-
IBMer and systems angel Marlene, who has organized me across many oceans and
continents, my dear wife-waft.

17.2 What It Was Like from the Inside

Others have presented many perspectives on my life and work, and now I'll tell how
it's been from the inside. I want you to know the whole story of the ideas I have tried
to carry out.

People now call me a "computer scientist." I did not think of myself as a computer scientist until recently, when people started calling me that, and Chapman
University made it official with their honorary PhD.

For most of my life I have thought of myself as a philosopher and a film-maker.

Note: Xanadu® and ZigZag® are registered trademarks of Project Xanadu. XanaduSpace™,
Zzogl™ and Utmos™ are claimed trademarks of Project Xanadu; and *transliterature* and *sworfing*
are offered as generic terms for some of these concepts.

T.H. Nelson (✉)
Project Xanadu, 3020 Bridgeway #295, 94965 Sausalito, CA, USA
e-mail: tandm@xanadu.net

© The Author(s) 2015

D.R. Dechow, D.C. Struppa (eds.), *Intertwingled*, History of Computing,
DOI 10.1007/978-3-319-16925-5_17

So I'll talk about philosophy and filmmaking—and media in general—before I talk about computers.

17.3   Philosophy of Intertwingularity

Let me begin at the philosophy end. Let's talk about intertwingularity.

This book, like the conference, is called *Intertwingled*. It's a word that expresses a philosophical position about cross-connection. I said in *Computer Lib* [2, 6], "Everything is deeply intertwingled." I meant that all subjects and issues are intertwined and intermingled.

But intertwingled subjects are not what computers usually represent. From the beginning, people have set computers up to be hierarchical. Hierarchy is not in the nature of the computer. It is in the nature of the people who set computers up.

If you say, "everything is hierarchical," as many computer people do, that is not science, it's a metaphysical position. It can't be proven true or false, it can only be proven inconvenient.

Hierarchy maps only some of the relationships in the world, and it badly maps the rest. You cannot represent history hierarchically, but as cross-connecting threads of narrative and relationship.

Unfortunately, the computer world has traditionally imposed hierarchy on everything. Most of the computer world is committed to a metaphysic of hierarchy. Files, directories, and now XML are hierarchical.[1] This is not just a philosophical position. It's an IMposition.

Now, it's also a metaphysic to say, "everything is deeply intertwingled," since the sentence cannot be proven true or false. But it is computer science to say that we need to represent cross-connection, and I'm expressing a computer science opinion when I say that intertwingularity is a better form of representation—for everything—than hierarchy. For things that overlap, shade off, and entwine, hierarchy does not work. Hierarchy is less and less appropriate as we try to represent more and more of the world.

Aristotle is often cited to support hierarchy. But intertwingularity has its philosopher too. His name was Heraclitus, and it was he who said you can never step in the same river twice, because of the constant flux of change and interconnection. Alas, none of his writing has survived, but his view of interconnection has.

My main designs, which I will discuss, are examples of intertwingularity. My document structure is cross-connective on the literary level, my data structure is cross-connective internally, and my viewing system is cross-connective on the screen.

This I see as practical intertwingularity.

---

[1] As well as the Document Object Model inside the browser, Cascading Style Sheets, tarballs and Zipfiles, LDAP, and much more.

17.4 Movies and the Other Presentational Arts

That is my brief on philosophy. Now let's talk about movies and media and presentational arts. This story is told at much greater length in POSSIPLEX [8].

The 1940s, the years of my boyhood, were media-rich. Usually, you experienced one medium at a time: magazines, radio, comics, stage and screen, and, of course, books. They all interested me much more than school or other kids. I drank in every aspect of every medium.

I adored the movies. (We lived in a very sophisticated part of Manhattan, so we saw more foreign movies than American.) I avidly studied the details of my comic books, from the language and visual angles to the dots of the color. And I listened to radio programs with every fiber of my brain.

I had four main media heroes in my first 10 years, and they are my heroes now: Walt Disney, Leonardo da Vinci, Frank Lloyd Wright, and Buckminster Fuller. They worked in different media, but in much the same way. Each was independent, visionary and original. All these years I have tried to be like them: independent, able to see what others could not, and creating new designs others could not imagine.

I also learned a lot about show business; I happened to have inside connections. I rarely saw my parents, who were divorced when I was born, but I learned a lot when I saw them. My mother became a star on Broadway in her twenties, and after she would take me to a Broadway play, she would take me backstage to meet the actors. My father was successful in another direction of show business. When I was ten, a new medium came along called "television," and he became a top director in that new medium. I got to sit behind him in control rooms at NBC and CBS.

I got to see how all that magic was made: on stage and TV, the technicalities and tricks, the pressure on the actors and crew, and the bravery in real time. I took some of that bravery with me when I started giving my radical speeches in the computer world, telling computer experts how their field should be conducted.

By the time I got to college my father had put me on TV, radio, and the professional stage—not much, but enough to be confident.

At Swarthmore College I became a media innovator. I had my own little magazine. The first issue I did jointly with my friend Len Corwin. I did the others by myself. I figured out how to use the new offset presses to print a magazine for 32 dollars. I commissioned the cartoons from a great cartoonist, Russ Ryan.

Figure 17.1 shows *Nothing #3*, a very mischievous design. It was kite-shaped, and it had to be rotated as you went from page to page. I did it when I was 19. It cost more than thirty-two dollars to print, but not much more. The printer, my friend Ned Pyle, approved the mockup, but he was astounded when he saw the result. I had done it on my own without realizing.

Later that year I wrote and directed what I believe was the first rock musical, *Anything & Everything*. It was a rock musical (a play in which actors would burst into song), not a "rock opera". But it had rock songs and a plot, and it came long before *Bye Bye Birdie* and *Hair*. Few have heard of it, but it ran at Swarthmore for two nights (as scheduled) in November of 1957. It is not in the official rock histories, but I think it should be.

Fig. 17.1 Issue #3 of *Nothing* magazine

Fig. 17.2 Still from *The Epiphany of Slocum Furlow*

My last year in college, I shot a 30-min comedy film, *The Epiphany of Slocum Furlow* (Fig. 17.2), which I think is the best thing I ever did. It is now available on YouTube. Because of the methods of that time, it took years to put the sound track on—not too well—but it tells a story and audiences laugh. I believe it shows that I was a competent film director from the start. I have never enjoyed any form of work so much.

Through all these lessons I came to learn that the presentational arts and media are all the same—writing, layout, diagrams, essays, poetry, and brochures; stage, screen, and radio. All these arts present ideas to the mind and heart with a variety of mechanisms, tricks of emphasis, sequence, and overview. And when we say "media" we simply mean the presentational arts as they get to be distributed in the world.

And in all these arts and media, the processes of designing and detailing are the same. Every part of every detail, in whatever medium, involves imagining how it will affect the heart and mind of the viewer (or reader, or participant, or user).

Movies are the pinnacle of the presentational arts because they bring together all the other modes—theater, graphics, sound, and more—with many, many mechanisms. Designing interaction was to be an inevitable new medium, requiring the same talents.

17.5   Loner

By the time I graduated from college, I was fearless and very ambitious. I expected to be a film director, but I also intended to be a *True Renaissance Man*, meaning a serious intellectual as well as a media guy. My professors had made it clear that I was good at philosophy, which I could not leave behind. So I graduated from college thinking of myself as a philosopher and filmmaker. Putting these together, I believed I could analyze anything, design anything, and see things others could not.

Collaboration was not my style. I'm not saying there's anything wrong with collaboration, but it has many drawbacks, especially if you have a large, precise vision. I have been criticized for citing mainly my own work. But I have found the work of others to be less and less relevant to my own.

17.6   My Plans

My plan out of college was to get a PhD and then go to Hollywood. Little did I know that grad school would be abrasive and boring, with no chance to do anything else.

But in graduate school I had a considerable epiphany (below), and I made a new and much bigger plan. I would found the personal computing industry and worldwide hypertext. I figured this might take until 1967, when I would be thirty; at which point I would get back to my original plan. (Note that Steve Jobs and Tim Berners-Lee were both 5 years old at this time, and they would have been eleven when I was thirty.)

I expected to make a lot of money in the computer field by that time. Meanwhile I would simply accumulate notes for my other projects, which I could then pay to have typed into the software I was designing. I would also have enough money to finance my own movies. And so I set aside—temporarily, I was sure—the one thing I really loved to do.

17.7 My Epiphany

Like Slocum Furlow, the hero of my college movie, I had an Epiphany. His was somewhat garbled. Mine was very clear (described in more detail in POSSIPLEX).
Sometime in the fall of 1960, I believe, I had the following premonitions:

- there would be a vast personal-computer industry;
- the future of human life and work would be at the interactive computer screen;
- the design of media for the interactive computer screen was in itself a worthy goal ("Screens!" I thought, "I can do THAT!");
- there would be a new medium of interactive text, which I envisioned as the true generalization of writing and literature (as humanity had known them for thousands of years), extending the medium far beyond the boundaries of paper; and
- it was my job to design this new medium, with whatever insights I already had about the overlap of subjects, the nature of the publishing industry, the sociology of readership, the different sides of copyright, and the nature of writing.

17.8 The Long March

I have worked hard on these matters for over 50 years since then, with great difficulty and little accomplished. Those who went after simpler goals, like Gates and Jobs and many lesser-known successes, had an easier time of it because they swam in a world of mutual agreement on conventional concepts. For instance, "word processing," a glorified typewriter, was simply for preparing conventional paper documents.

I see the purpose of computers as giving us new and better worlds, not simulating the old. The others were content to build conventional tools, not radical ones, and they were not hell-bent to use them for radical new media, as I was.

This is not the place to talk about adventures or people or badly chosen fights, partly enumerated in my autobiography. I have worked on overarching designs very different from what others have done, and I have disagreed with almost everybody about almost everything in the fields of personal computing and electronic documents.

Meanwhile, I have hundreds of thousands of notes from these 54 years, possibly a million. Figure 17.3 shows a tray of my file cards. It contains computer notes from the 1960s, sorted by topics of my own devising. I kept all my notes on file cards until the 1980s, and then I went to various forms of chronological pages and books. It would be nice to work out a chronology of my work, but very difficult and time-consuming.

Because I have disagreed with almost everybody about almost everything, it was a special miracle to find my five collaborators in 1979, discussed below.

Fig. 17.3 A tray of file-card notes from the 1960s

17.9   Seeking the Magic

In design, I believe in magic. That is to say, there can be magical combinations and configurations that are not obvious—simple ideas that extend to create an elegant unified system. An example that moved me as a boy was Wright's legendary house, Fallingwater. In high school I was similarly moved by several electronic designs: heterodyning, the Theremin, and the Hammond Organ. In the computer field, I was greatly inspired by several different pieces of software and hardware: the APL computer programming language; the PDP-8 computer; Ivan Sutherland's Sketchpad; Ken Knowlton's L6 language; Nassi-Shneiderman diagrams; and Sinden's film, *Force, Mass and Motion*.

Their designers had all found simple constructs that generated all the results they wanted. This was a clear lesson for the design of software—finding the cleanest and most powerful constructs.

Constructs are the heart of the computer. In general, computers do not deal with reality. Computers deal with constructs. The constructs we put into the computer then become the computer's model the world. Files and directories are constructs. Screen windows are constructs. *Word processor* and *spreadsheet* are constructs.

As I said above, I see the purpose of computers as giving us new and better worlds, not simulating the old. This meant envisioning new worlds and finding new constructs to generate these new worlds cleanly.

Designing constructs—what I call Construct Logic—is for me the center of software design. Trying to find the magical, minimal structure is the highest goal. As in

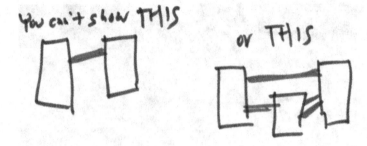

Fig. 17.4 What can't be shown on the Web or with other electronic documents

those examples that moved me in my youth, I have sought construct designs that had elegance, minimalism, and generative power. This was a new kind of philosophical design—the design of abstraction.

Over this half century of work, I believe I have found the cleanest and most general designs for interactive systems. These satisfy a lot of people's wish lists, but with very simple and unifying structures.

Each of these designs is nonhierarchical and intertwingled.

I believe I have found a system of documents far deeper, and a system of data far richer, and a system of visualization far more sweeping, than proposed by those others who imitated the past. To work on anything else seems wrong to me, for I still must get these things working.

17.10   Preamble to Xanalogical Documents: What's Wrong with the Web?

People keep asking me, "What's wrong with the World Wide Web?"

What's wrong with the Web is—to begin with—the same thing that's wrong with Microsoft Word and paper simulation in general. You can't show parallel pages, visibly connected (Fig. 17.4).

This is not just a complaint about the Web. It's a complaint about the simulation of paper by computer. It is my complaint about textfiles, Microsoft Word, and PDF: all are systems of paper simulation that cannot show parallel pages visibly connected!

17.11   Seeking the True Generalization of Literature: Translit/Xanalogical Structure (Trademarked *Xanadu*)

As I said before, I see the purpose of computers as giving us new and better worlds, not simulating the old.

I asked this in 1960: If we could interact with documents on screens, what would be the truest, finest generalization of literature? This was a philosophical question with a powerful kick, for it defined the way we might be able to think in the future. Indeed, "As We May Think" [1] was the title of an article that had influenced me as a boy.

But what abstractions and generalizations to choose? The new document design should be elegant. It should be comprised of the simplest possible constructs.

I then realized that the screens of the whole world would be connected, and my aspirations exploded further. To redefine the whole of literature, with new capabilities making it grander and far better, seemed to me the truly noble ambition to which I must turn.

My document design began with the idea of managing my notes on a computer screen, and setting it up so that the same note could combine with others in different ways, the different combinations visible side by side. This meant indirect addressing, now called *transclusion*, which I believe was one of my earliest ideas.

And I immediately imagined the document structure of the future, including the jump-links of today's Web, but with certain key differences.

While most of this design came to me in 1960–1961, it took a long time— 18 years—and working with five brilliant collaborators (Roger Gregory, Mark S. Miller, Stuart Greene, Roland King, and Eric C. Hill), to reconcile all the parts into a clean internal structure,[2] which we call xanalogical hypertext, or Translit. The system has been described in the original conference paper [11] and in the various editions of *Literary Machines* [3, 5].

The document structure turned out to be very difficult for people to understand. Many people read Literary Machines, even the simple classic edition [3], and couldn't understand it at all. In fact, without a visible example, most people of that time couldn't even imagine jump-links.

17.12 Transpointing Windows

In hindsight, I should have simply emphasized a non-abstract aspect that people could visualize: "parallel pages, visibly connected on the screen." Even at that time, a few people might have been able to imagine it. But I left it out of my earlier papers, thinking it was obvious. I first published the concept in a 1972 paper for a conference I couldn't afford to attend [10]. I didn't have a computer at the time—no individuals did—so I simulated it on top of a Selectric typewriter, to demonstrate parallel pages and windows visibly connected (Figs. 17.5 and 17.6). In more recent writings I have called these transpointing windows. [4, 7].

---

[2]In brief: Indirection, assembling a document from designated portions; visible transclusion, meaning the origin context of each portion available next to the new context; links as first-class, addressable objects; links attached to contents by their original addresses; and the micropurchase of content where necessary.

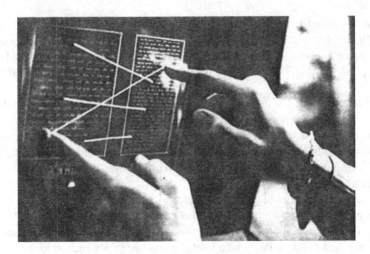

Fig. 17.5 Simulated computer screen created to demonstrate, "parallel pages, visibly connected"

Fig. 17.6 Simulated
computer screen built by the
author, ca. 1971

But the world started to go in a different direction. In the 1970s, the current
windowing system was adopted by Macintosh and Windows. While the current windowing system is often referred to as "the GUI" (Graphical User Interface) or "the
PUI" (PARC User Interface), it is highly restrictive. As implemented at Apple and

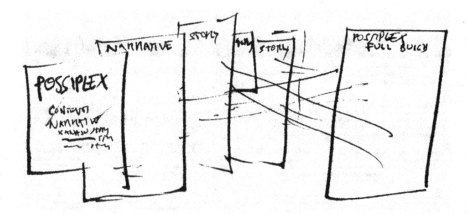

Fig. 17.7 Notional rearrangement of my autobiography, POSSIPLEX, into parallel connected pages

Microsoft, it completely prevents the kind of connection illustrated in Figs. 17.5 and 17.6 and those that follow.[3]

I must stress this to listeners over and over. Today's operating systems rule out interconnection between windows at the system level—only within a restricted "application" can such windows be interconnected, and only if you create a new set of windows internal to the application. Of course, one sneaky method is to seize the whole screen as a transparent canvas, but this still does not give access to the windows provided by the operating system.

It is still hard for many people to understand that I mean actually showing visible connections between pages on the screen, and hard for them to imagine writing based on this capability, though it is the only kind of writing I wish to do. For instance, I would like to rewrite my autobiography into parallel, visibly connected pages, in case I have the time and tools to do so (Fig. 17.7).

17.13 Xanalogical Structure

The document structure we designed in 1979, xanalogical structure, has been greatly set back by events. However, several interactive demos of xanalogical documents have been implemented.

The first interactive version we can now show was "The Ping Demo," done by Ka-Ping Yee in 1999 (Fig. 17.8). It shows (and scrolls) two versions of Jefferson's

---

[3] I have been assured by Alan Kay that the original PARC design, as implemented in his original Smalltalk at PARC, would have allowed visible connections between windows, but that the narrowness of the Apple, Microsoft, and Linux implementations of the PARC User Interface will not allow such connection.

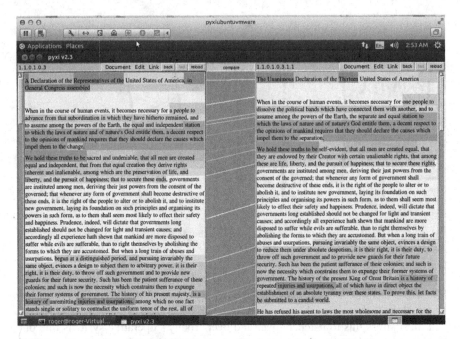

Fig. 17.8 The Ping Demo: Interactive xanalogical implementation by Ka-Ping Yee

Declaration of Independence. Fed by the Xanadu Green server, it shows transclusions but no xanalinks.

The most recent instantiation of xanalogical structure is OpenXanadu, implemented by Nicholas Levin in April 2014 (Fig. 17.9). It runs in a browser, and it also shows only transclusions but no xanalinks. The document illustrated is "Origins," by Moe Juste. Note that the entire King James Bible is in the left-hand column.

Our most general and vivid xanalogical presentation is the XanaduSpace demo, which was programmed by Robert Adamson Smith in 2007. This demonstration shows connected, parallel pages in a 3D space (Fig. 17.10). The document illustrated is again, "Origins," by Moe Juste. This version shows both transclusions and xanalinks.

Another version of transpointing windows is CosmicBook from 2003 (Fig. 17.11). This version is not xanalogical. It is a simple hypertext with visible links.

These different versions of transpointing windows show the implementability of the concept, though they are still regrettably far from product.

17.14 Our Other Intertwingled Software

While xanalogical/transliterary documents have been the center of my concern, I have also worked on other forms of cross-connected software, two in particular.

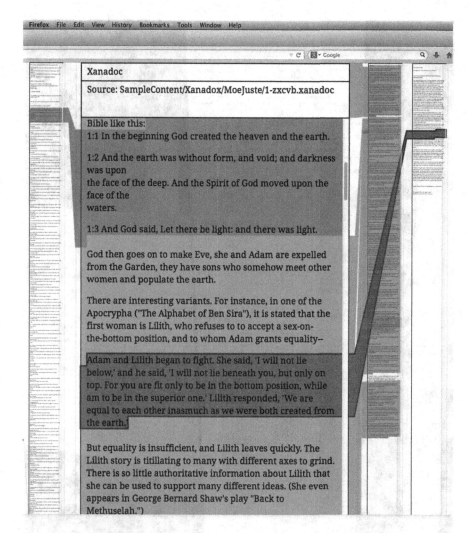

Firefox   File   Edit   View   History   Bookmarks   Tools   Window   Help

Xanadoc

Source: SampleContent/Xanadox/MoeJuste/1-zxcvb.xanadoc

Bible like this:

1:1 In the beginning God created the heaven and the earth.

1:2 And the earth was without form, and void; and darkness was upon
the face of the deep. And the Spirit of God moved upon the face of the
waters.

1:3 And God said, Let there be light: and there was light.

God then goes on to make Eve, she and Adam are expelled
from the Garden, they have sons who somehow meet other
women and populate the earth.

There are interesting variants. For instance, in one of the
Apocrypha ("The Alphabet of Ben Sira"), it is stated that the
first woman is Lilith, who refuses to to accept a sex-on-
the-bottom position, and to whom Adam grants equality--

Adam and Lilith began to fight. She said, 'I will not lie
below,' and he said, 'I will not lie beneath you, but only on
top. For you are fit only to be in the bottom position, while
am to be in the superior one.' Lilith responded, 'We are
equal to each other inasmuch as we were both created from
the earth.'

But equality is insufficient, and Lilith leaves quickly. The
Lilith story is titillating to many with different axes to grind.
There is so little authoritative information about Lilith that
she can be used to support many different ideas. (She even
appears in George Bernard Shaw's play "Back to
Methuselah.")

Fig. 17.9 Parallel connected pages in the OpenXanadu browser implementation

17.14.1   Spreadsheet and Database Intertwingled in a Single Construct (Hyperthogonal Structure, Trademarked ZigZag)

In 1982, I realized that spreadsheet cells and database fields could be reduced to a single, minimalist construct—a cell connectable into crossed lists, or zzcell.

Conventional spreadsheets and databases can be built from zzcells, but so can other powerful structures harder to describe, crisscrossed in multiple ways at right angles ("hyperthogonal").

Fig. 17.10 Parallel connected pages in the XanaduSpace demo, implemented by Robert Adamson Smith, 2014

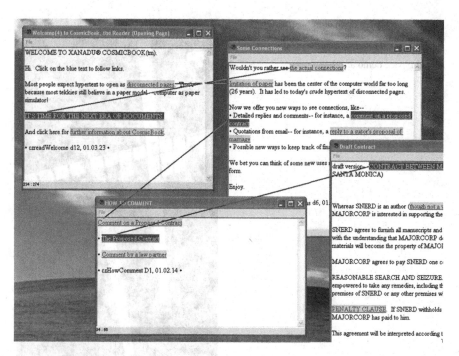

Fig. 17.11 CosmicBook, programmed by Ian Heath

This cell, the zzcell, is a curious construct. It is a unit that can be cross-connected in orthogonal dimensions. But these are not spatial or Cartesian dimensions, they are just listing dimensions, and the links are merely precedence links (Fig. 17.12).

This has many consequences, consequences that are presented at the ZigZag home page [9]. That page also enumerates the different versions of ZigZag and the people who deserve credit for building them.

17.14.2 The Most Generalized Mutidimensional Graphics Engine

Conventional software deals with 2D objects (conventional electronic documents and tables) and 3D objects ("virtual reality" and CAD models).

Based on these other mechanisms, we have a graphics engine that does animated tweening in a multidimensional coordinate space. Thus, it is in principle the most general viewer. We call such tweening *sworfing*, since it can do either swooping or morphing.

This viewer (called Zzogl in its one instantiation) appears to work very well. However, it has only been exercised in three dimensions.

Fig. 17.12 Hyperthogonal
cells shown in 3D. The
internal mechanisms of the
XanaduSpace demo are
shown

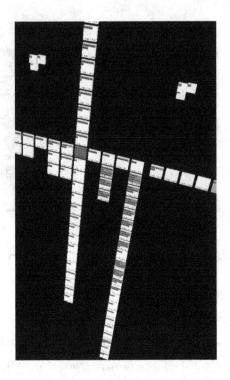

The viewer creates—that is, interactively presents—a viewing space of which all other viewing spaces are subsets. We may think of such N-dimensional Cartesian spaces as a generalization of "virtual reality." But since it can also do front-to-back occlusions like conventional PUI windows, which are called 2½D (a term for which I thank Ron Baecker), this viewer may be said to allow N½D viewing. This viewer, then, may and should be used as a visualization substrate for everything else.

17.15   Merging the Generalizations: Generalized Documents, Data Cells, and Viewer

I have enumerated three fundamental designs, each of which I believe is the cleanest and most general possible design in its field:

- Documents: xanalogical documents
- Database and Spreadsheet: hyperthogonal data cells
- Visualization: a multidimensional engine for arbitrary new spaces

How to fit these systems together is not determinate. Each of them is a construct system that generates a universe with its own rules.

Each of them is useful on its own, but I envision a single user environment built from all three—an everyday workspace offering documents and visualizations not otherwise possible. The hardest design problem I have faced is making these constructs fit together into a single clean system. I believe I have succeeded, but there is no room for the solution here. The problem now is to make it work.

17.16   Not in the Box

Thinking out of the box never meant anything to me because I never got into any box. I grew up in Greenwich Village and conventionality never appealed to me. I have tried to skip the obvious and find the magic.

In the computer world I have from the beginning considered myself an alternative school of thought, as if I were a university on another planet, not trapped in the ideas of the rest of the computer world. I've been a Free Range intellectual, outside the chicken-wire of academic departments and traditions that powerfully shape the thoughts of those who seek tenure.

Why? From an early age I was accustomed to having insights others did not dare to imagine. It has been my job to tell the truths people don't want to hear.

17.17   Today's Prison

My religion is human freedom and human creativity.

I dreamt of a liberating system of personal computing; instead we now have a computer world of imprisonment and imposition. I dreamt of a new liberating medium of hypertext that would make people smarter; that dream has turned into a flapping, screaming mess that slathers content with special effects and panders to the lowest minds.

I consider today's computer world a nightmare honkytonk prison. From boyhood until college, school to me was imprisonment and imposition, and these same issues now define the computer world—imprisonment and imposition. So my course has been unchanged straight on till now.

17.18   Conclusion

What I intended to do in 1961 was done by others, but divided among Jobs, Gates, and Berners-Lee, all of whom did it wrong.

I inspired a lot of people with my book *Computer Lib*, but this gives me no joy, since what they did, and the way they did it, would have happened anyway. My anomalous position in the computer revolution parallels that of Hugh Hefner in the sexual revolution—each of us triggered, idealized, and publicized a revolution that was inevitable. Except Hefner was really conventional, though he didn't know it.

Whereas my vision for the computing revolution has been far from the conventional. In decades of thinking and searching, I believe I have found the cleanest and most general designs for all interactive systems, each nonhierarchical and intertwingled—a system of documents far deeper, a system of data far richer, and a system of visualization far more sweeping, than proposed by those others who imitated the past. To work on anything else seems wrong to me, for I still must get these things working.

Control freak? I prefer the term "artist." In the computer world I consider myself an *artist of construct design*, and I believe my constructs still hold great promise.

I believe this would be a much better world if I had succeeded. But I ain't dead yet.

References

1. Bush V (1945) As we may think. Atlantic 176:101–108
2. Nelson TH (1974) Computer Lib: you can and must understand computers now/dream machines. Hugo's Book Service, Chicago
3. Nelson TH (1981) Literary machines: the report on, and of, Project Xanadu concerning word processing, electronic publishing, hypertext, thinkertoys, tomorrow's intellectual revolution, and certain other topics including knowledge, education and freedom. Theodor H. Nelson, Swarthmore
4. Nelson TH (1995) The heart of connection: hypermedia unified transclusion. Commun ACM 38(8):31–33
5. Nelson TH (1985) Literary machines, (85.1 technical edn). Mindful Press, Swarthmore
6. Nelson TH (1987) Computer Lib: you can and must understand computers now/dream machines, Rev and updated edn. Tempus Books of Microsoft Press, Redmond
7. Nelson TH (1998) Parallel visualization: transpointing windows. Project Xanadu. http://xanadu.com.au/ted/TN/PARALUNE/paraviz.html
8. Nelson TH (2010) POSSIPLEX: movies, intellect, creative control, my computer life and the fight for civilization: an autobiography of Ted Nelson. Mindful Press, Hackettstown; distributed by Lulu.com. http://www.lulu.com/shop/ted-nelson/possiplex/ebook/product-17533977.html
9. Nelson TH (2011) The ZigZag® Database and visualization system. Project Xanadu. http://xanadu.com/zigzag
10. Nelson TH (1972) As we will think. Online 72: international conference on online interactive computing. Brunel University, Uxbridge, pp 439–454
11. Nelson TH (1980) Replacing the printed word: a complete literary system. In: Information processing 80: proceedings of IFIP congress 80. IFIP congress series 8. North-Holland Publishing, Amsterdam, pp 1013–1023